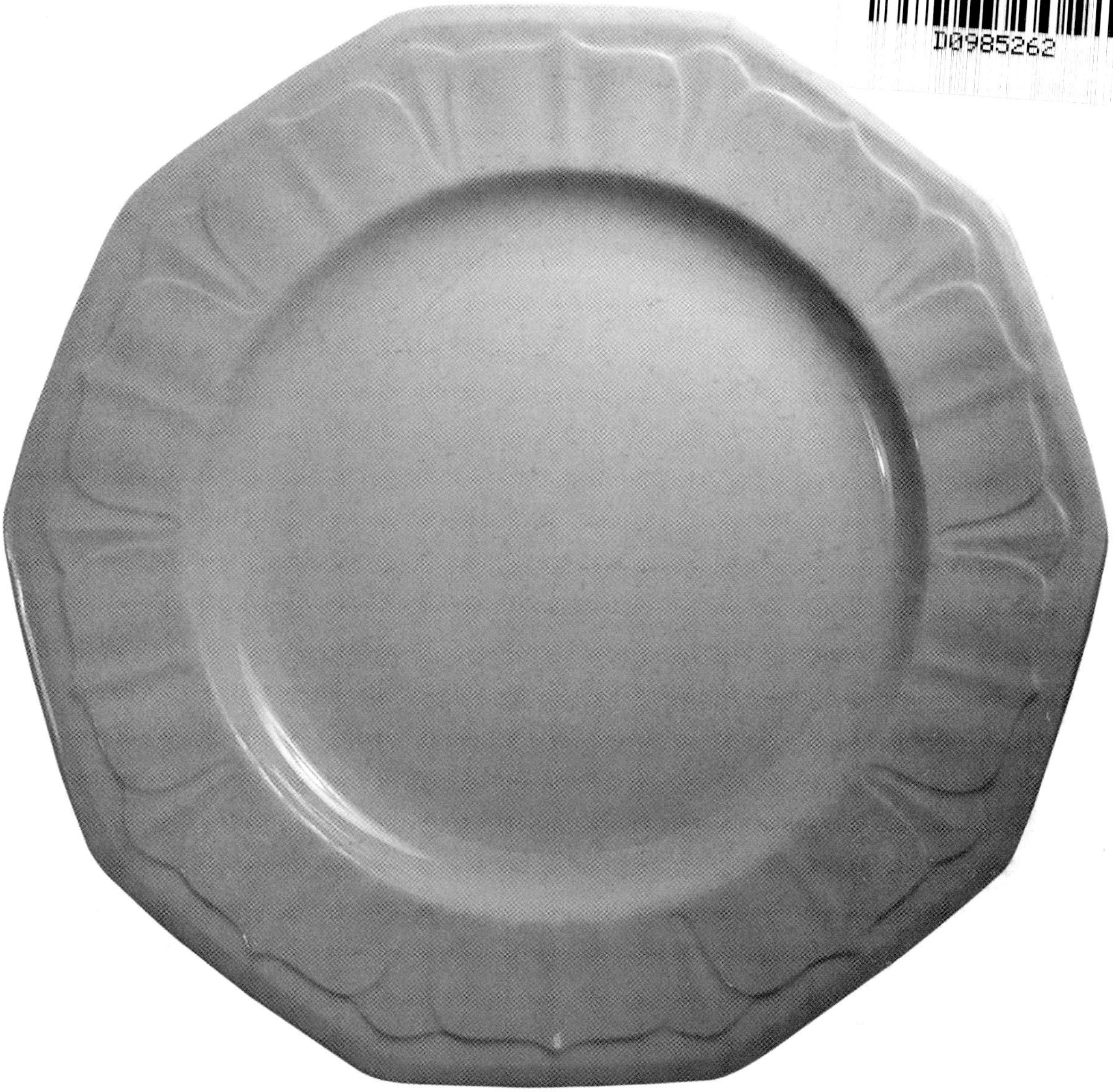

White Ironstone China

Plate Identification Guide 1840-1890

Ernie and Bev Dieringer

4880 Lower Valley Road, Atglen, PA 19310 USA

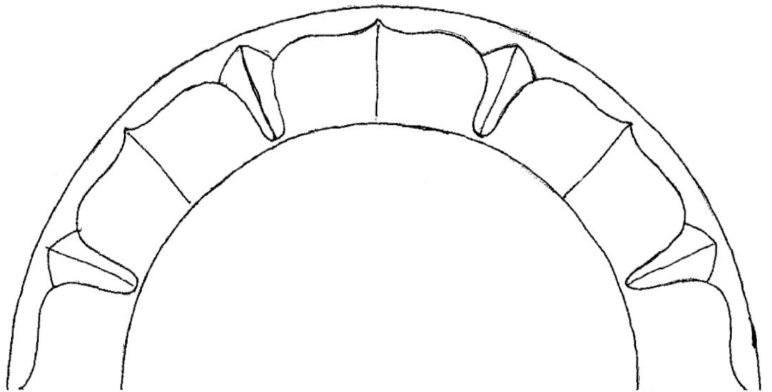

Library of Congress Cataloging-in-Publication Data

Dieringer, Ernie
White ironstone china: plate identification guide, 1840-1880/Ernie and Bev Dieringer.
p. cm.
ISBN 0-7643-1227-8
1. Ironstone china--Catalogs. 2. Pottery--19th century--England--Catalogs. I. Dieringer, Bev. II. Title.
NK4367.17 D54 2001
738.3'0942'09034--dc21
00-011040

Designed by "Sue"
Type set in Geometric 231 Hv BT/Aldine 721 BT

ISBN: 0-7643-1227-8
Printed in China
1 2 3 4

Published by Schiffer Publishing Ltd.
4880 Lower Valley Road
Atglen, PA 19310
Phone: (610) 593-1777; Fax: (610) 593-2002
E-mail: Schifferbk@aol.com
Please visit our web site catalog at
www.schifferbooks.com
We are always looking for people to write books on new and related subjects.
If you have an idea for a book, please contact us at the above address.

This book may be purchased from the publisher.
Include $3.95 for shipping. Please try your bookstore first.
You may write for a free catalog.

In Europe, Schiffer books are distributed by
Bushwood Books
6 Marksbury Ave. Kew Gardens
Surrey TW9 4JF England
Phone: 44 (0)20 8392-8585; Fax: 44 (0)20 8392-9876
E-mail: Bushwd@aol.com
Free postage in the UK. Europe: air mail at cost.
Please try your bookstore first.

Contents

Acknowledgments

Wally Skinner's plates stacked and ready for drawings to be made of the embossed designs.

We give special thanks to John Wallace "Wally" Skinner, whose extensive collection of over ninety white ironstone china plates forms the basis of this study. Also, we are very grateful to Howard and Sally Erdman who shared their large collection and sent over fifty plates from Texas to Connecticut so that we could photograph them. Our sincere thanks goes to Dale Abrams for his generosity and hospitality, enabling us to add fifteen shapes and information about copper lustre shapes, which is included as one of the sections. We are grateful for the editing skills of Harriet Denton and Jim and Mara Kerr. Jean Wetherbee was a great source of information and research. She helped assemble the marks shown here; she has been gathering backmarks for many years. We thank her also for editing this manuscript. Grateful thanks also go to Janet and Jack Allers, Jane and Wes Diemer, Carol Fleischman, Polly Gosselin, Frances Hills, Kathy and Tom Lautenschlager, Anne and Jim Miller, Tom and Olga Moreland, Dorothy and Howard Noble, Maureen Oliver, Shirley and Ira Parmer, Julie and Roxann Rich, Sarah Schutte, Ray and Ellen Secrist, Diane Stocki, Nancy Upchurch, Bertica Vasseur, Liz Volckening, Eleanor Washburn, and John and Jane Yunginger.

Introduction

The idea for this book began with John Wallace Skinner of Cleveland, Ohio, who has collected plates since 1954. He generously made available his photos and information to start the process of gathering as many patterns as could be found. Jean Wetherbee, author of *White Ironstone: A Collector's Guide,* believes there are more than three hundred shape names; however, some shapes have several names, so there may not be quite that many different plates. All of the shapes known to have been made have not been found, and more are discovered every year, but this study contains the shapes that were produced in large quantities by potteries in England for export to the American market between 1840 and 1890. Research on twentieth century shapes and makers is left for others to complete.

With the information contained herein, the identification of unmarked white ironstone plates is possible. Loosely organized by characteristics, the shapes are arranged so that identification can be made from common design elements: plain round, many sided, florals, leaves, etc. There are designs that span several categories and some that have more than one name. The Index of Shape Names will help those who are looking for a particular shape. If only the potter's name is known, the Index of Potters will locate the pages of shapes on which the potter is mentioned and his work is illustrated.

One can be certain of a shape's identification only when a plate is clearly marked with a printed or impressed diamond registry symbol. Those shapes listed with a name and the word "Shape" are names given by the maker at the time of registry. J.F. (Jacob Furnival), J. & G. Meakin, and Pankhurst are three potters who rarely registered their shapes; therefore, their original shape names are generally not known, but names have been assigned to their shapes over the years by serious collectors and researchers as a means of identification and communication. A drawing of each plate has been included, and some of the impressed marks have been drawn, for clarity. Lustre decorated plates are used to illustrate a shape only when a white plate was not available. There is a section by Dale Abrams devoted to Copper Lustre and Tea Leaf decorated ironstone, including identification charts and body shapes and motifs.

Back marks are included wherever possible. There may be others, as well, because research indicates that there were hundreds of potteries working in England during the last quarter of the 19th century that may have made white ironstone for export to the American market.

Keys to the Diamond Registry Mark

KEY TO YEAR AND MONTH LETTERS ON DIAMOND REGISTRY MARKS

1842-67 Year Letter at Top		1868-83 Year Letter at Right		Months (Both Periods)
A = 1845	N = 1864	A = 1871	L = 1882	A = December
B = 1858	O = 1862	C = 1870	O = 1877	B = October
C = 1844	P = 1851	D = 1878	S = 1875	C or O = January
D = 1852	Q = 1866	E = 1881	U = 1874	D = September
E = 1855	R = 1861	F = 1873	V = 1876	E = May
F = 1847	S = 1849	H = 1869	W = Mar. 1-6 1878	G = February
G = 1863	T = 1867	I = 1872		H = April
H = 1843	U = 1848	J = 1880	X = 1868	I = July
I = 1846	V = 1850	K = 1883	Y = 1879	K = November (and December 1860)
J = 1854	W = 1865			M = June
K = 1857	X = 1842			R = August (and Sept. 1st-19th, 1857)
L = 1856	Y = 1853			W = March
M = 1859	Z = 1860			

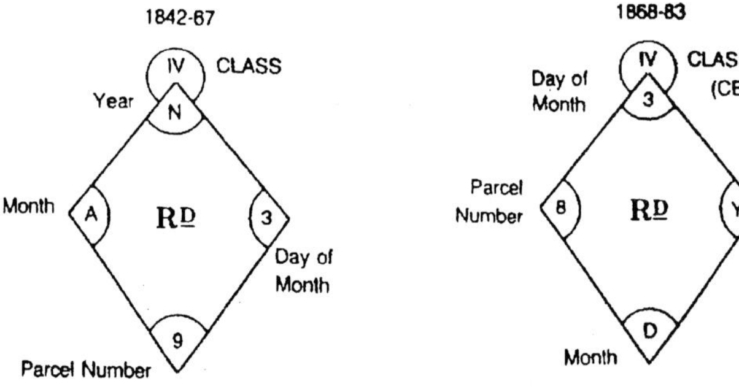

Plate Parts

Webster's *Dictionary* defines "plate" as a shallow dish, usually circular, from which food is eaten. Plates are the most common item of ceramic manufacture. They are, along with cups, essential containers from which people eat and drink. Plates refer to flat servers less than twelve inches in diameter; those represented here are between nine and ten and one half inches in diameter.

Plates, whether round, octagonal, or other, have a flat well with a relatively flat brim. This shape is an English fashion, in contrast to the Chinese fashion which was shaped like a large saucer without a brim. The brim derives from the shapes of English pewter plates that were sent to China in the sixteenth century to be copied in ceramics during the East India trade. The brim was called a condiment brim, and was used for salt, mustard, relish, or whatever else was used to enhance the flavors of food.

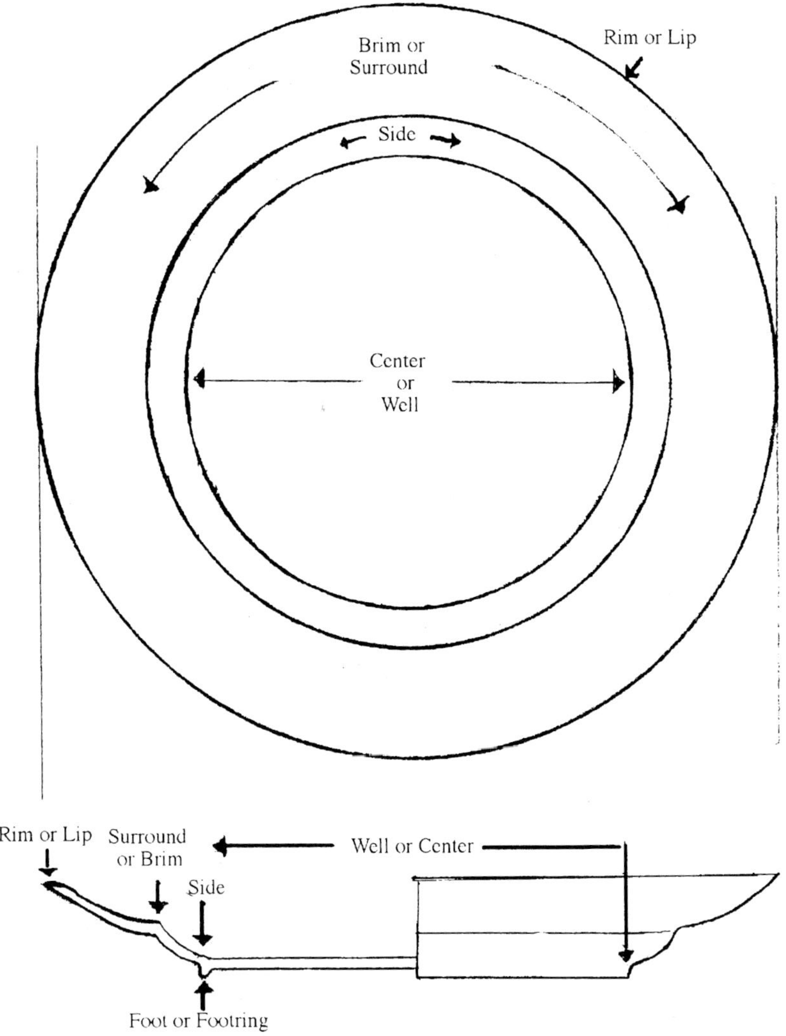

White Ironstone Shapes

Plain Round

The plain round shape was made by so many English potteries in the mid-nineteenth century that one plate is shown here to represent them all. Plain round plates have subtle differences in their weights, thicknesses, sharpness of their edges, and widths of the surrounds. These have no embossed lines, raised edges, or borders. Examples include the Sevres, Union, and plain Berlin shapes.

Gothic
Cockson & Chetwynd, Cobridge
1867-75
(Subsequently Cockson & Seddon 1875-77)
The shape name Gothic, should not be confused with the earlier, sided shapes.

1850 to early 1870s

Shape Name	Potter	Registration Date
Classic Shape	T. & R. Boote	Reg. Jan. 8, 1868
Crystal	Elsmore & Forster	
Erie Shape	Wedgwood & Co.	Reg. by E. & D. Chetwynd (modeler) Jan. 21, 1867
Fanfare	Elsmore & Forster	
Fig Cousin	Davenport/Wedgwood	Reg. July 14, 1853
Grenade Shape	T. & R. Boote	Reg. Dec. 8, 1858
Havre Shape	John Edwards	Reg. June 12, 1866
Pear	A. Shaw	
Plain Scallop	see Crystal Shape above	
Plain Uplift	Clementson Bros.	
	Cockson, Chetwynd & Co.	Reg. Jan. 7, 1868
	Maddock, later Maddock & Gator	Reg. June 12, 1875
	Alfred Meakin	
Richelieu Shape	J. F. Wileman	
Rondeau	Davenport	
Senate Shape	T. & R. Boote	Reg. Sept. 26, 1870

Late 1870s and 1880s

Shape Name	Potter
American	Powell & Bishop
Bar & Chain	J. Maddock & Co.
Berlin Shape	Mellor, Taylor & Co.
Britannia	Powell & Bishop
Cable & Ring	Various Potters
Chain of Tulips	J. & G. Meakin
Clover	Cockson & Seddon
Eagle	Cockson & Chetwynd
Florence (impressed)	Henry Alcock & Co.
Gothic (impressed)	Cockson & Chetwynd
Hexagon Strap	Bridgwood & Son
Late Tulip	Wedgwood & Co.
Lion's Head	Mellor, Taylor & Co.
Oxford	Henry Alcock & Co.
Plain	Baker & Chetwynd
	Burgess & Goddard (exporter)
	Cockson & Seddon
	Edward Clarke
	Gelson Bros.
	George Jones
	Grose & Co.
	Henry Burgess
	Mellor, Taylor & Co.
	Old Hall E'Ware Co., Ltd. (Formerly Charles Meigh)
	Thomas Hughes
	Thomas Elsmore
	Wedgwood & Co.
	Wood & Hawthorn
Royal (Prince of Wales)	John Edwards
	Burgess & Goddard (exporter)
Seine	John Edwards
Simplicity	Burgess & Goddard
Simplicity	Maddock & Co.
Victory (Dolphin)	John Edwards

Backmarks

Following are as many backmarks as could be found with the help of Jean Wetherbee, who has been gathering these marks for years. There may be many that are not included here because research tell us there were hundreds of potters in England making white ironstone ceramics, especially during the last quarter of the nineteenth century.

Some of the marks found on plain white plates

ROYALSTONE CHINA
WEDGWOOD & CO.
ENGLAND

ROYAL STONE CHINA
WEDGWOOD & Co

WEDGWOOD & CO
Rd
ERIE SHAPE

TRADE MARK
WEDGWOOD & Co
ENGLAND

TRADE MARK
WEDGWOOD & Co

STONE CHINA
J.W. PANKHURST & Co
HANLEY
ENGLAND

ROYAL IRONSTONE CHINA
JOHNSON BROS
LATE PANKHURST & Co
ENGLAND

ROYAL IRONSTONE CHINA
JOHNSON BROS
ENGLAND

IMPERIAL
IRONSTONE CHINA
COCKSON & SEDDON

IRONSTONE CHINA
V R
J. & G. MEAKIN
ENGLAND

IRONSTONE CHINA
J. & G. MEAKIN
HANLEY
ENGLAN

ROYAL IRONSTONE CHINA
ALFRED MEAKIN
ENGLAND

IRONSTONE CHINA
J & G. MEAKIN.

IRONSTONE CHINA
SOL
REGD 391413
J&G MEAKIN
ENGLAND

IRONSTONE CHINA
JAMES F WILEMAN

WARRANTED
IRONSTONE CHINA
TRADE MARK
JOHN EDWARDS
ENGLAND

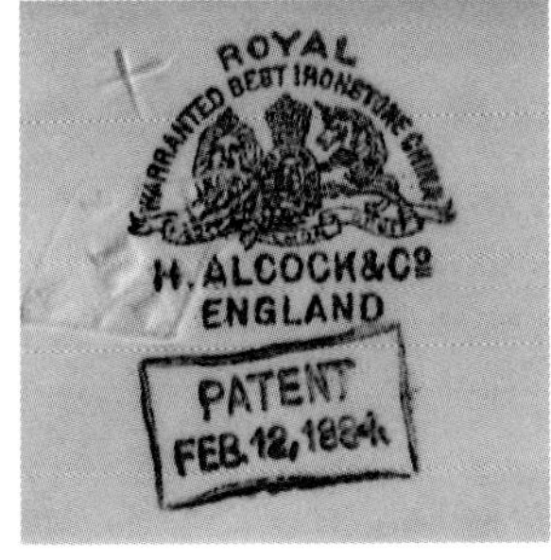
ROYAL
WARRANTED BEST IRONSTONE CHINA
H. ALCOCK & Co
ENGLAND
PATENT
FEB. 12, 1884

IMPERIAL
IRONSTONE CHINA

IMPERIAL IRONSTONE CHINA
WARRANTED
RICHARD ALCOCK
BURSLEM ENGLAND

ROYAL IRONSTONE CHINA
A. J. WILKINSON
ENGLAND

OPAQUE STONE CHINA
TRADE MARK
ANTHONY SHAW & SON
ENGLAND

STONE CHINA
H. BURGESS. BURSLEM.

MADDOCK & GATER
TRADE MARK
STAFFORDSHIRE POTTERIES

IRONSTONE
CHINA
BISHOP & STONIER
ENGLAND

Plain Berlin
Liddle Elliot & Son, Longport
Reg. April 21, 1864
Skinner collection

Sevres Shape
John Edwards, Fenton
1853 – 1860
Skinner collection

Heath's Unknown
(6 divisions)
J. Heath, Tunstall
Reg. 1853

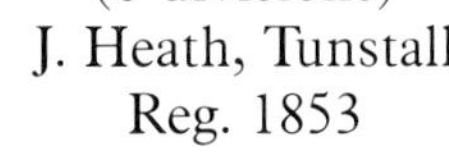

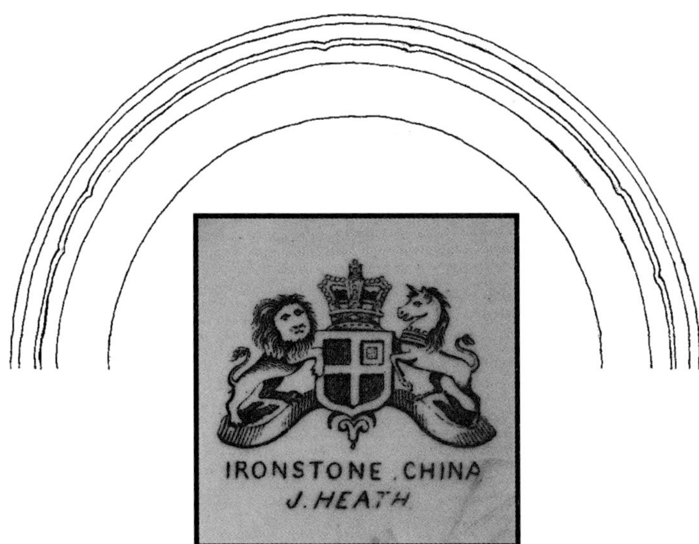

Union Shape
T. & R. Boote
Reg. Aug, 22, 1856
Diemer collection

Early Round

Triple Border
(6 divisions)
James Edwards, Dale Hall
1842 – 1851
Noble collection

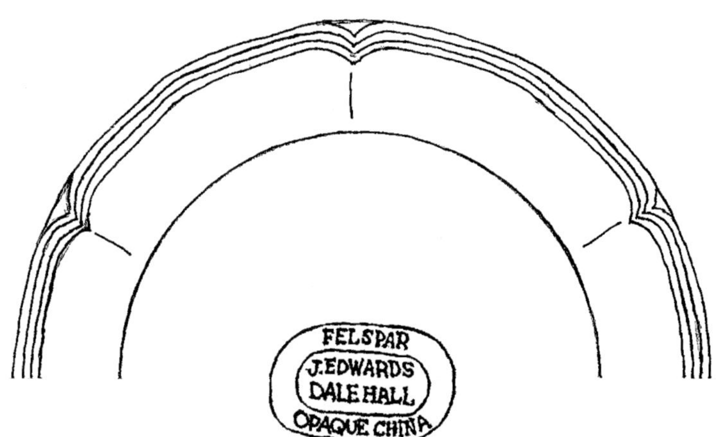

Triple Border
(6 divisions)
E. & C. Challinor
1862 – 1891
Skinner collection

Ball and Stick
(8 divisions)
James Edwards, Dale Hall
1842 – 1851
Skinner collection

Walled Octagon
(8 divisions)
J.F.
1845-1870
Washburn collection
Can be found with
Lustre Band
decoration

Early Sided

Curved Gothic
(8 sided)
James Edwards
Reg. Aug. 30, 1843
Pat. #9678
Skinner collection

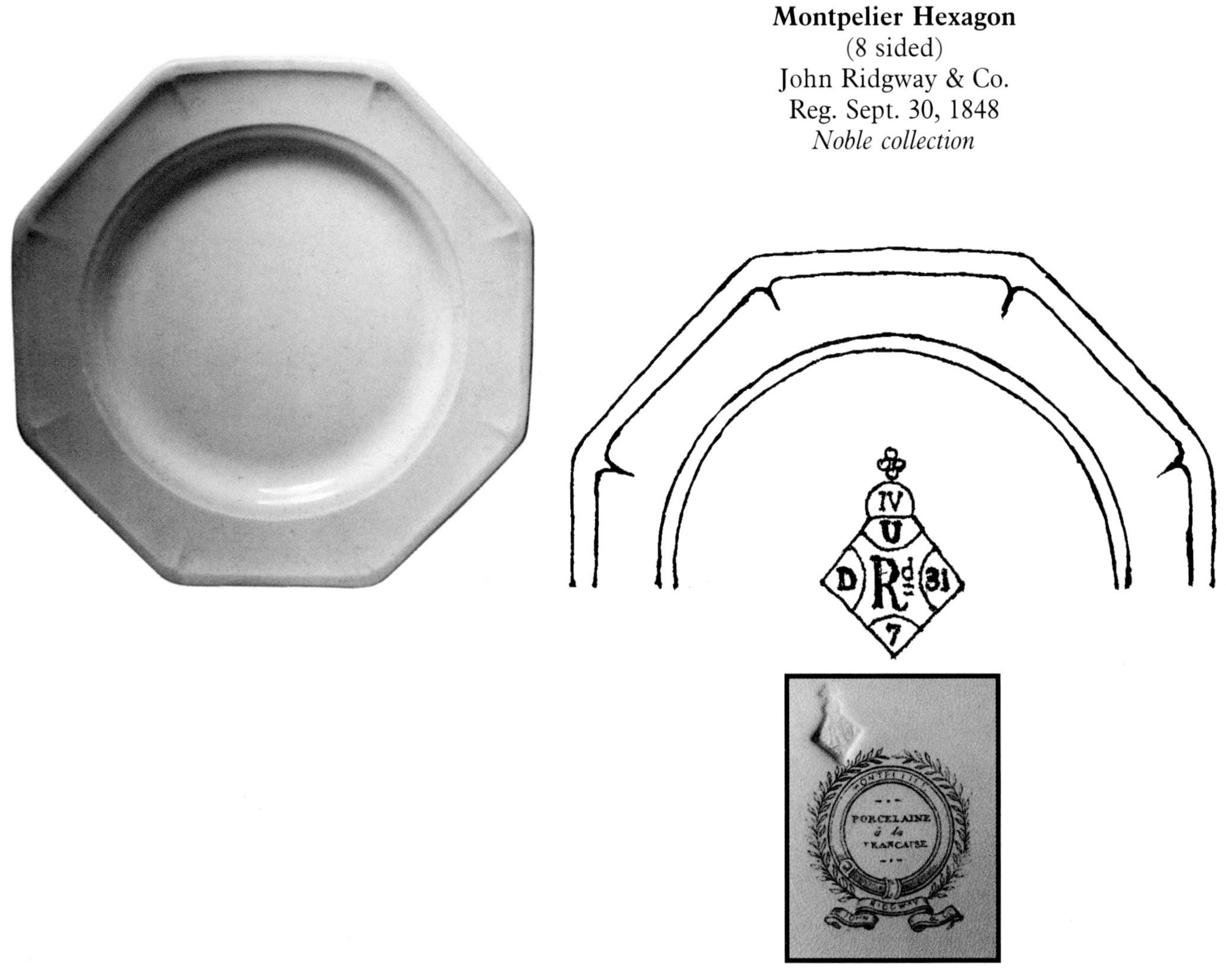

Montpelier Hexagon
(8 sided)
John Ridgway & Co.
Reg. Sept. 30, 1848
Noble collection

Morley's Gothic
(10 sided)
F. Morley & Co, Shelton
1845 – 1858
Brownfield's Gothic
William Brownfield & Son
After 1871 of an 1840s Shape
Noble collection

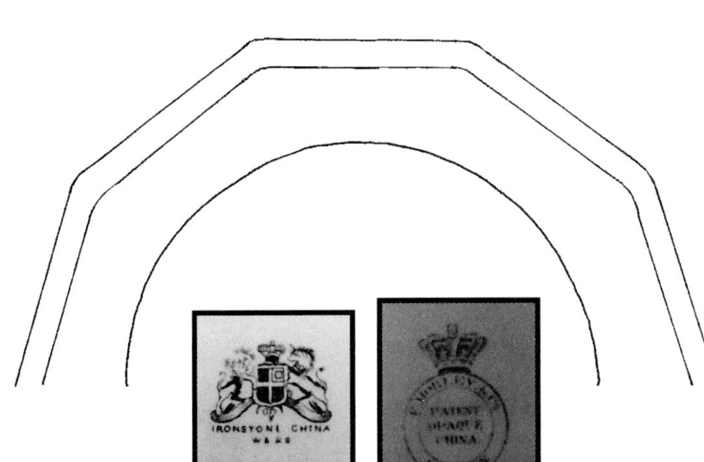

Boote's Gothic
(10 sided)
T. & R. Boote, Burslem
1842 – 1850
Skinner collection

Gothic
(12 sided with inverted ribs and walled rim)
c. 1840s
I. Meir & Son
W. & G. Harding, Burslem
C. & W. K. Harvey
Skinner collection

John Alcock
Sml Alcock
C. Meigh & Sons
Edward Walley
Noble collection
Can be found with
Teaberry Lustre
Lustre Band
Tea Leaf Lustre (on Walley)
Pinwheel Lustre
Scallop Lustre
Thistle & Berry Lustre
decoration

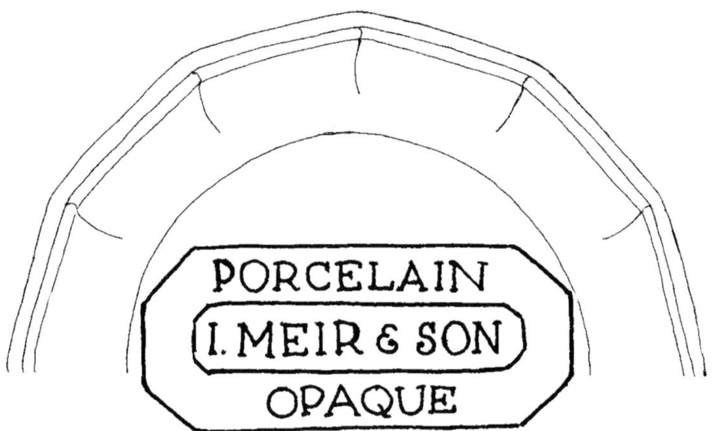

Gothic
(12 sided with everted ribs and embossed lines on rim)
c. 1840s
W. Adams & Sons
E. Challinor & Co.
John Alcock
T. Goodfellow, Tunstall
J. Heath
John May, Tunstall
E. Walley
(Note: there is no dating in the John May diamond)
Skinner collection

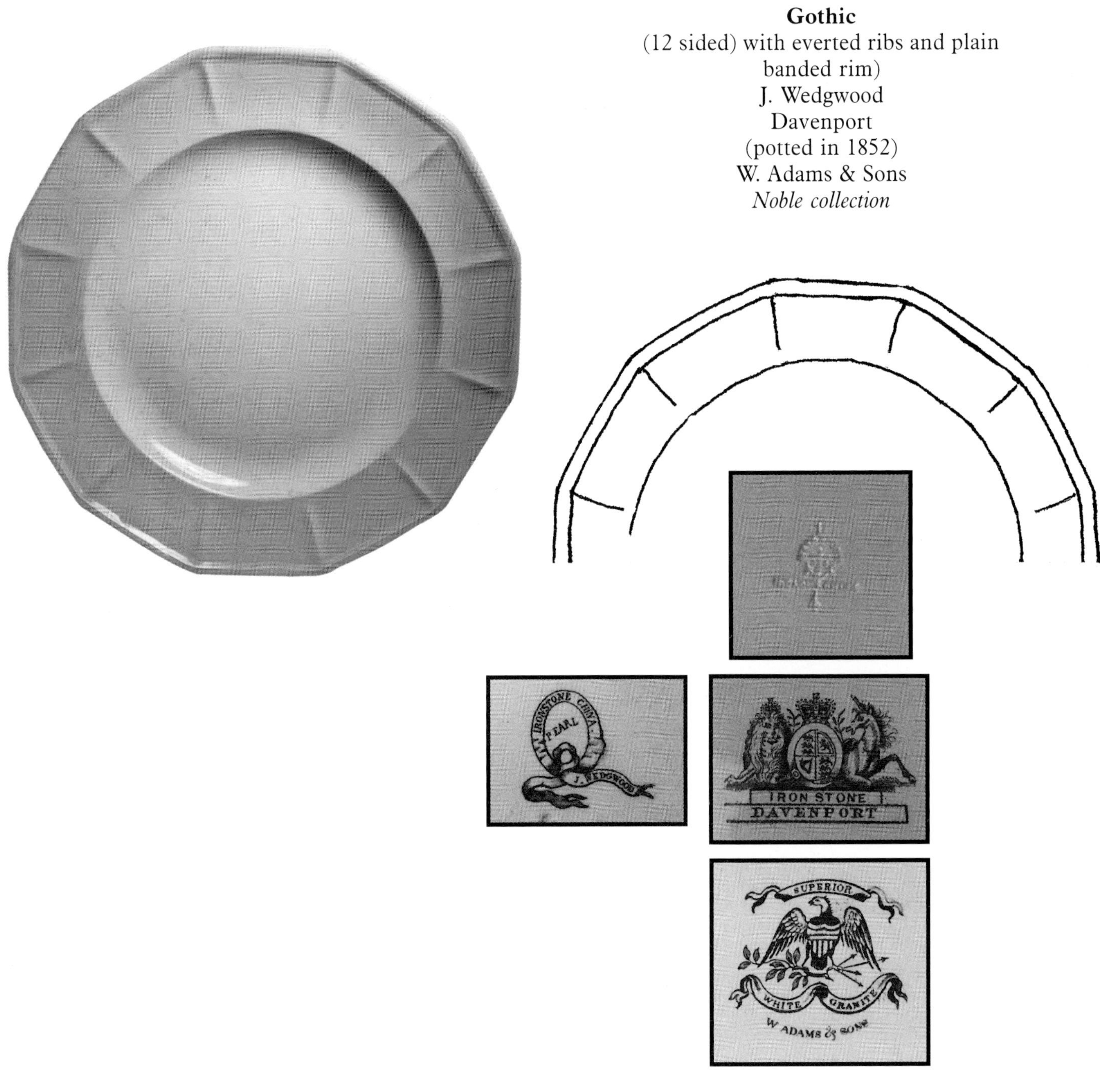

Gothic
(12 sided) with everted ribs and plain banded rim)
J. Wedgwood
Davenport
(potted in 1852)
W. Adams & Sons
Noble collection

Berlin Gothic
(14 sided)
T. J. & J. Mayer
c. Early 1840s
Dieringer collection

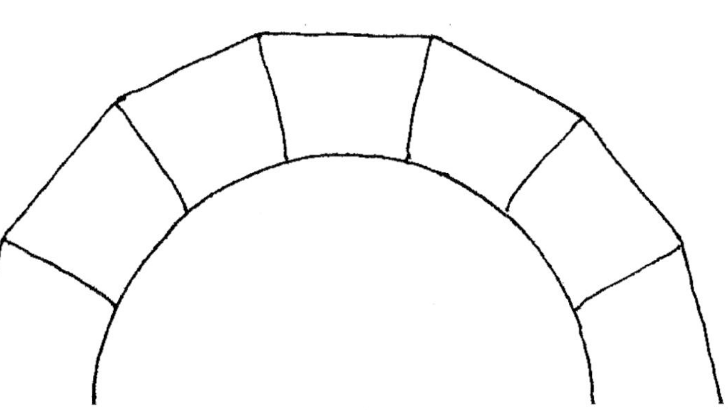

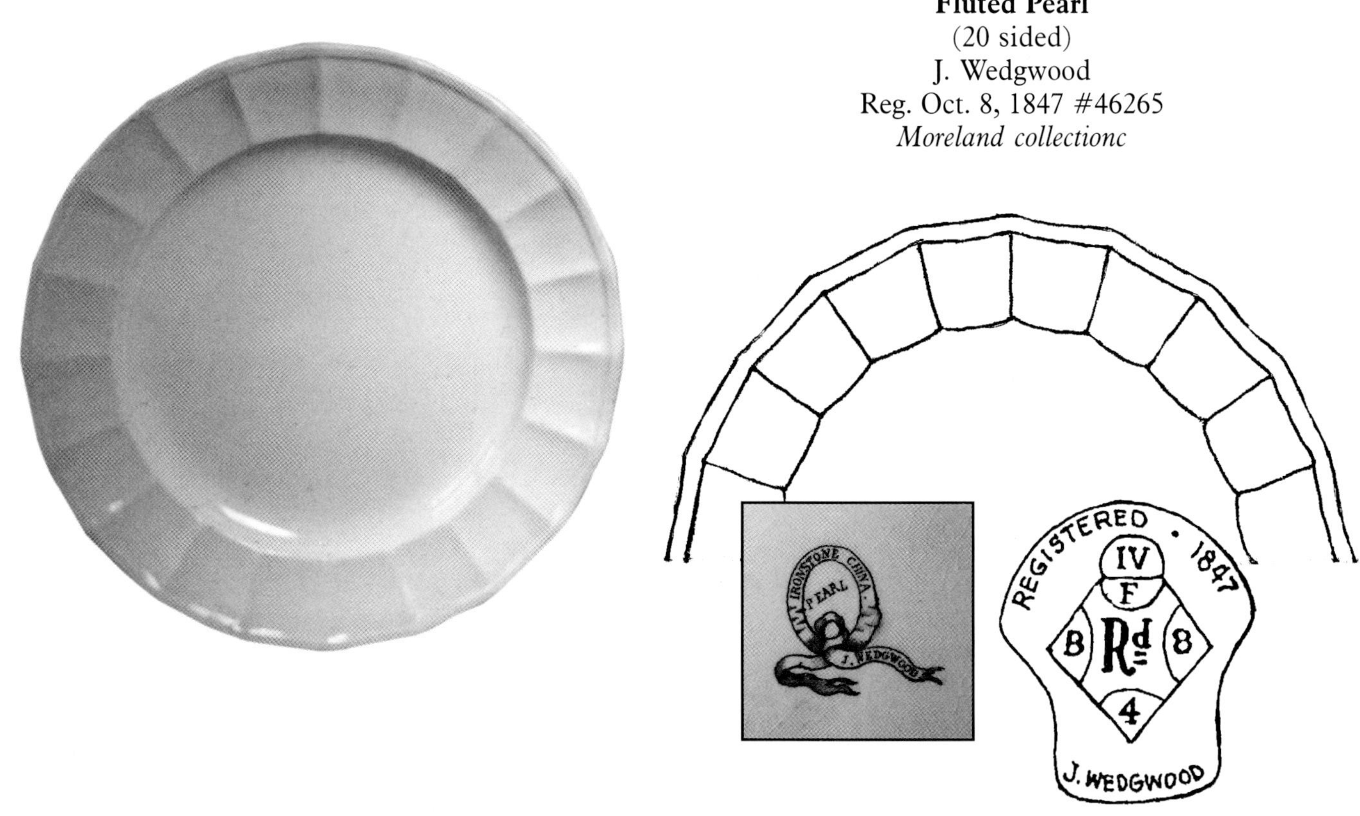

Fluted Pearl
(20 sided)
J. Wedgwood
Reg. Oct. 8, 1847 #46265
Moreland collectionc

Ridgway/Morley's Unnamed
(16 sided)
Ridgway & Morley, Shelton
1842 – 1844
Noble collection

Chinese Shape
(16 divisions)
T. & R. Boote
Reg. Dec. 8, 1858
John Alcock, Cobridge
c. 1850
Hills collection

J. Clementson (with copper lustre Teaberry)
Abrams collection
(Also see Shaw's Chinese)

Can be found with
Tea Leaf Lustre
Teaberry Lustre
Lustre Band
Other Lustre
decoration

DeSoto Shape
(10 divisions – 20 sided)
Stephen Hughes & Son, Burslem
Thomas Hughes, Reg. Apr. 17, 1855
Skinner collection

Can be found with
Tea Leaf Lustre
Lustre Band
decoration

Grape Octagon
(10 sided)
Samuel Alcock
Barrow & Co.
Brougham & Mayer
E. Challinor & Co.
J. Clementson
E. Corn
Freakley & Farrall
J.F. c. 1845
J. & R. Goodwin
J. W. Harris
Hulme & Booth
Livesley & Powell
Pearson & Hancock
Venables, Mann & Co.
E. Walley
Thomas Walker
Moreland collection

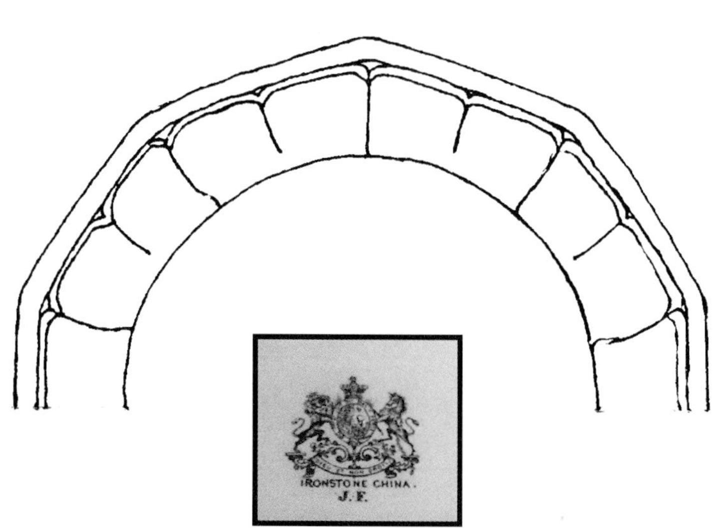

Can be found with
Teaberry Lustre
Lustre Band
Pinwheel Lustre
Pomegranate Lustre
Pre-Tea Leaf Lustre
Scallops Lustre
Thistle & Berry Lustre
Other Lustre
decoration

Scallop

True Scallop
(14 sided)
James Edwards
c. 1845
J.F.
T. & R. Boote
E. Walley
Skinner collection

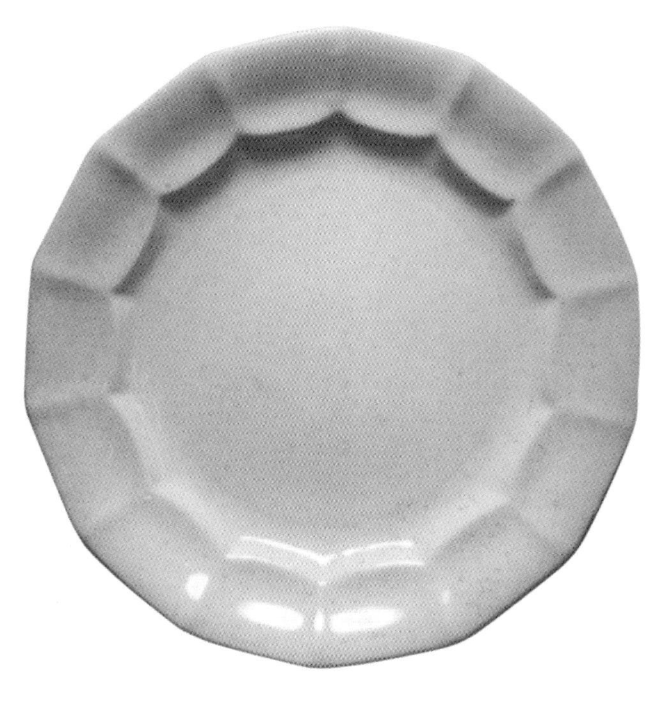

Round Scallop
(14 divisions)
c. 1845
James Edwards
E. & C. Challinor
John Alcock
I. (John) Meir & Son
Jacob Furnival
Skinner collection
G. Wooliscroft
Noble collection
J. Clementson
(with Teaberry)
Abrams collection

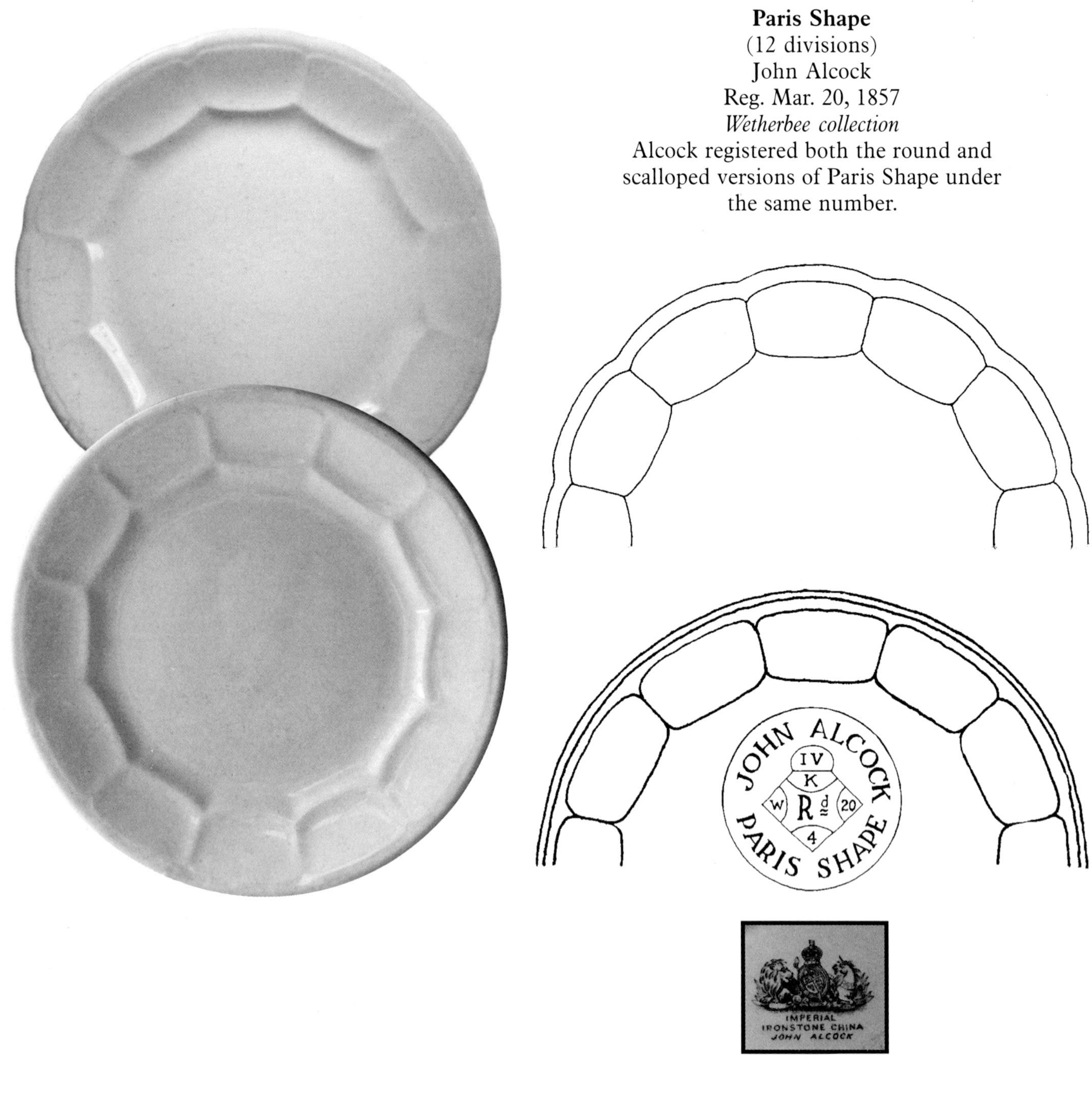

Paris Shape
(12 divisions)
John Alcock
Reg. Mar. 20, 1857
Wetherbee collection
Alcock registered both the round and scalloped versions of Paris Shape under the same number.

Portland Shape
(12 divisions)
Two versions
Elsmore & Forster
c. 1860
Hills collection

Portland Shape
(12 divisions)
Elsmore & Forster
c. 1869
Diamond collection

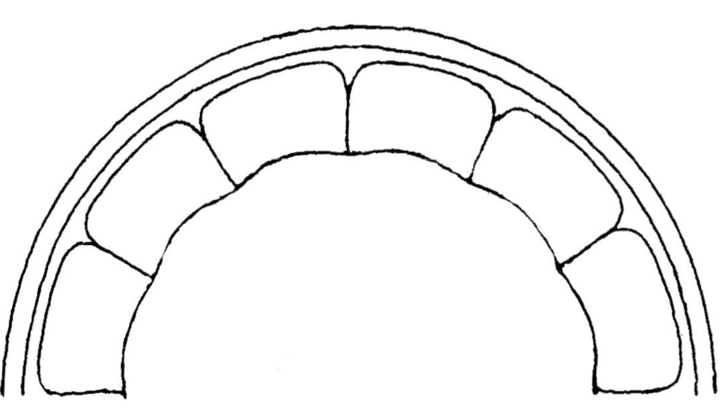

Portland Shape
(10 divisions)
Elsmore & Forster & Co.
1853-1871
Abrams collection
Can be found with
Lustre Band
Reverse Teaberry Lustre
Morning Glory Lustre
decoration

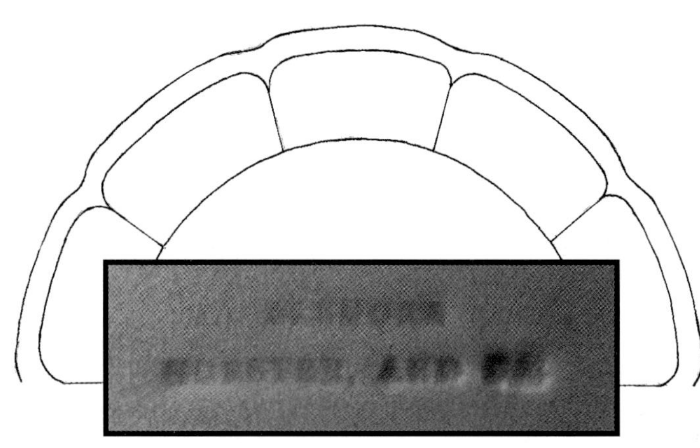

Mayer's Classic
(12 divisions)
T. J. & J. Mayer
c. 1847
Hills collection

Pankhurst's Unnamed Shape
(4 divisions)
J. W. Pankhurst & Co., Hanley
1852-1882
Skinner collection

Arch or Loop

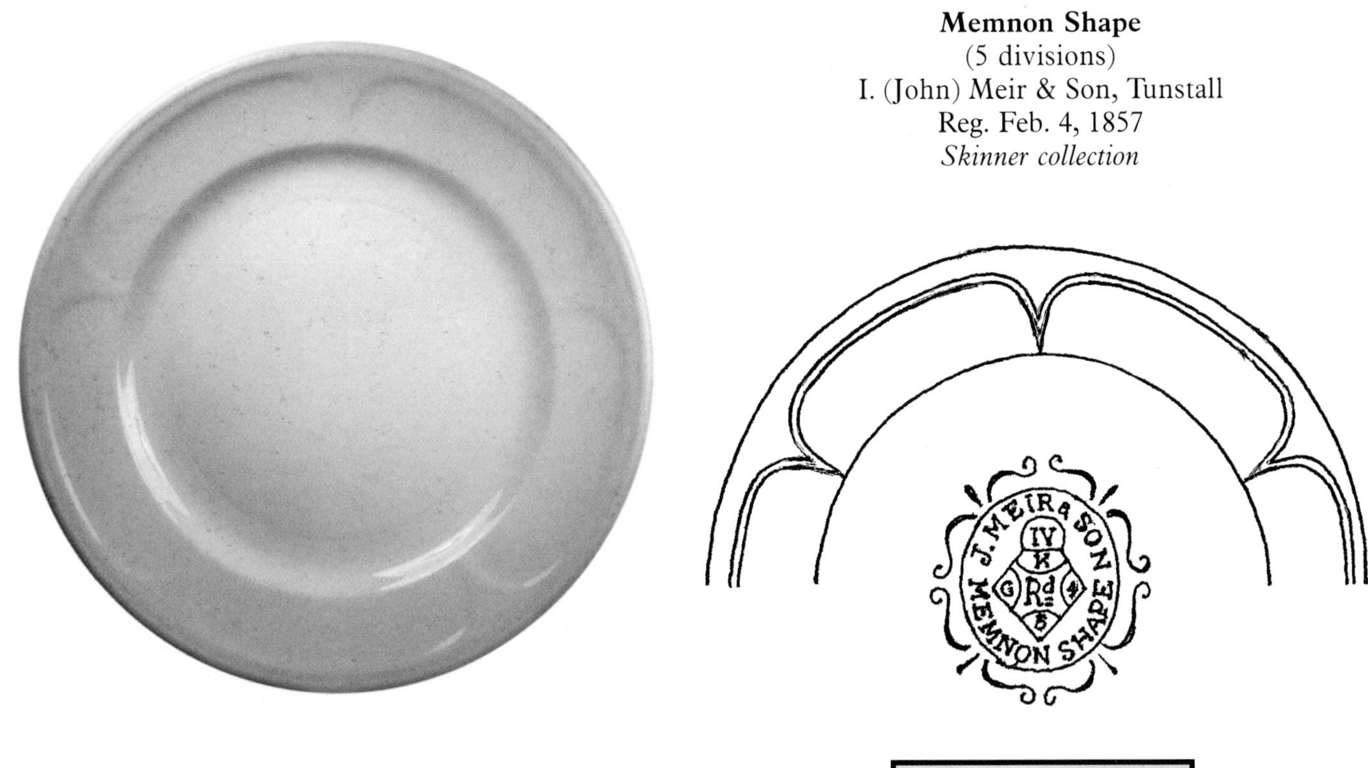

Memnon Shape
(5 divisions)
I. (John) Meir & Son, Tunstall
Reg. Feb. 4, 1857
Skinner collection

Quartered Rose
(6 divisions)
Liddle Elliot & Son
Jacob Furnival
1845-1870
Lautenschlager collection

Can be found with
Teaberry
Lustre Band
Pinwheel Lustre
Other Lustre
decoration

Split Pod
(8 alternate divisions)
James Edwards & Son, Dale Hall
Reg. Aug. 8, 1855
Hills collection

Alternate Loops
(8 alternate divisions)
Bridgwood & Clarke, Burslem
1857 – 1864
Hills collection

Scragg's Unnamed Shape
(8 divisions)
Reg. Oct. 11, 1853 by Ralph Scragg (Modeler)
Potted by Beardmore & Dawson, Longton
In business only four months.
Dieringer collection

Augusta Shape
(10 divisions)
J. Clementson, Shelton
1848-1864
Abrams collection

Can be found with
Teaberry Lustre
Lustre Band
decoration

Shaw's Chinese
(10 divisions)
Anthony Shaw, Burslem
J. Clementson
Reg. April 7, 1856
Skinner collection
(Also see Chinese Shape)

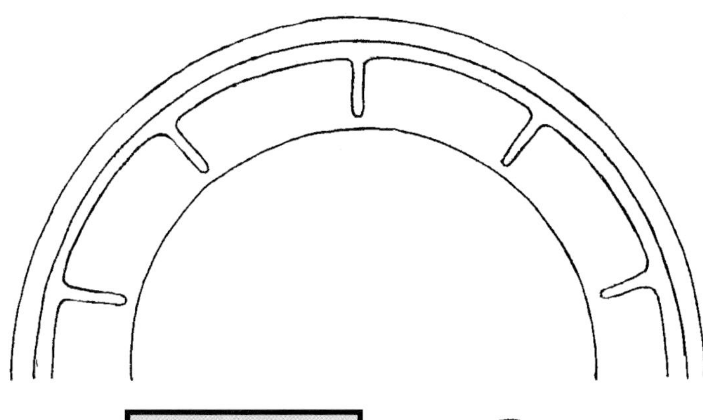

Can be found with
Tea Leaf Lustre
Teaberry Lustre
Other Lustre decoration

Framed Panels
(10 divisions)
C. Meigh & Son
1850-1861
Erdman collection

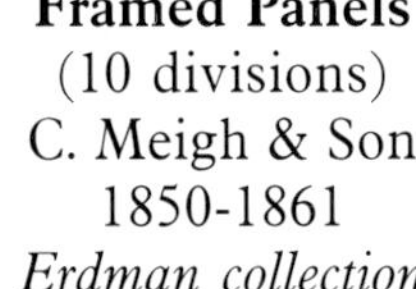

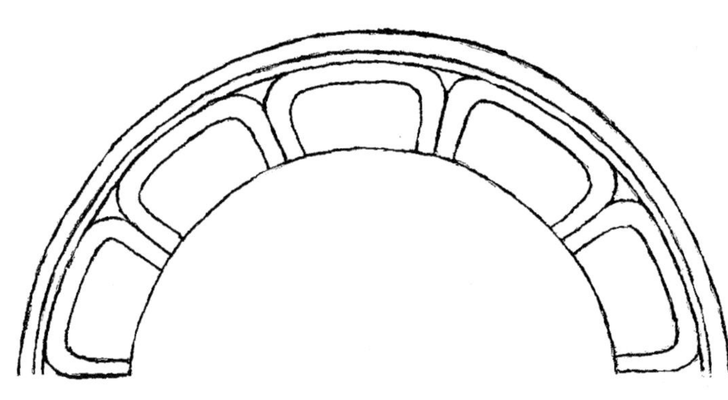

Virginia Shape (Decagon)
Brougham & Mayer, Tunstall
Reg. June 15, 1855
Moreland collection

Virginia Shape (Round)
Brougham & Mayer, Tunstall
Reg. June 15, 1855
Skinner collection

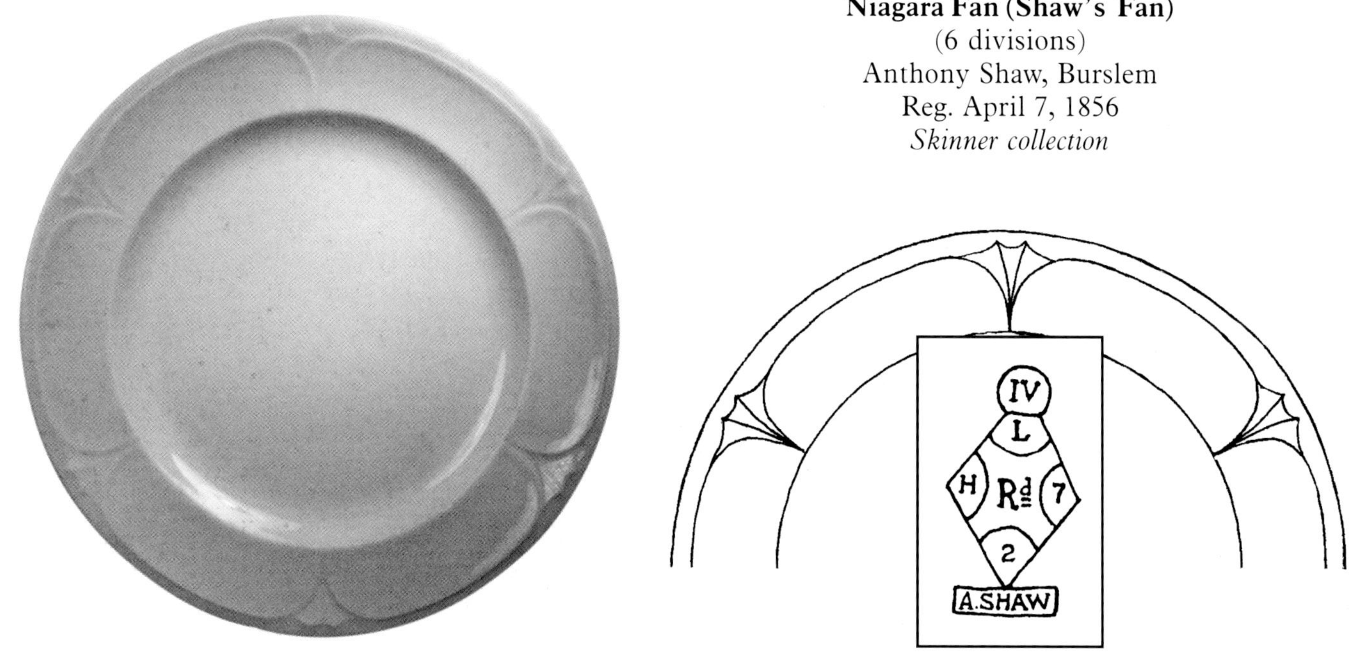

Niagara Fan (Shaw's Fan)
(6 divisions)
Anthony Shaw, Burslem
Reg. April 7, 1856
Skinner collection

Can be found with
Tea Leaf Lustre
Lustre Band
decoration

Niagara Shape
(5 divisions)
Edward Walley, Cobridge
Reg. Nov. 29, 1856
Washburn collection

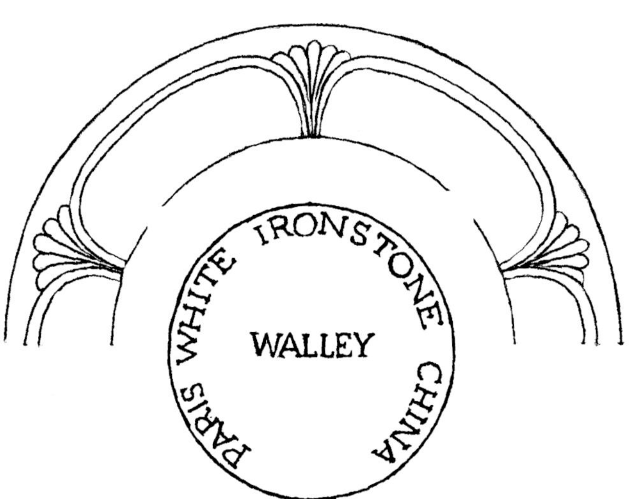

Can be found with
Lustre Band
Pinwheel Lustre
Pomegranate Lustre
Pre-Tea Leaf Lustre
Other Lustre decoration

Berry Cluster
(6 divisions)
Jacob Furnival
1845 – 1870
Abrams collection

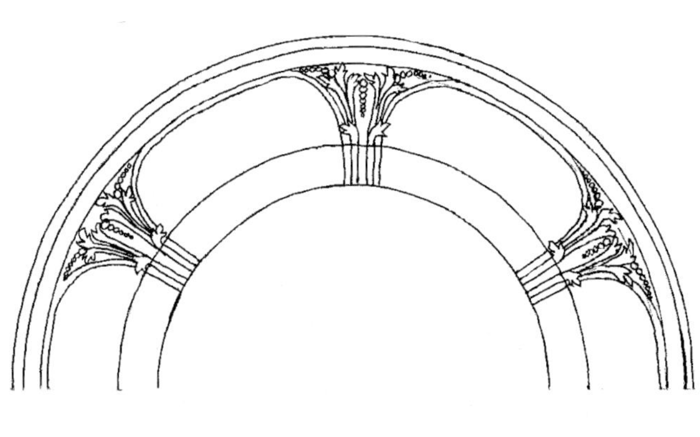

Can be found with
Teaberry Lustre
Lustre Band
Chelsea Grape Lustre
decoration

Venables' Unnamed
(6 divisions)
John Venables & Co., Burslem
Trent Pottery
1853 – 1855
Miller collection

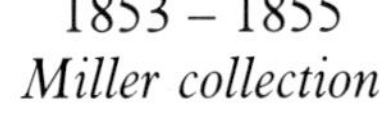

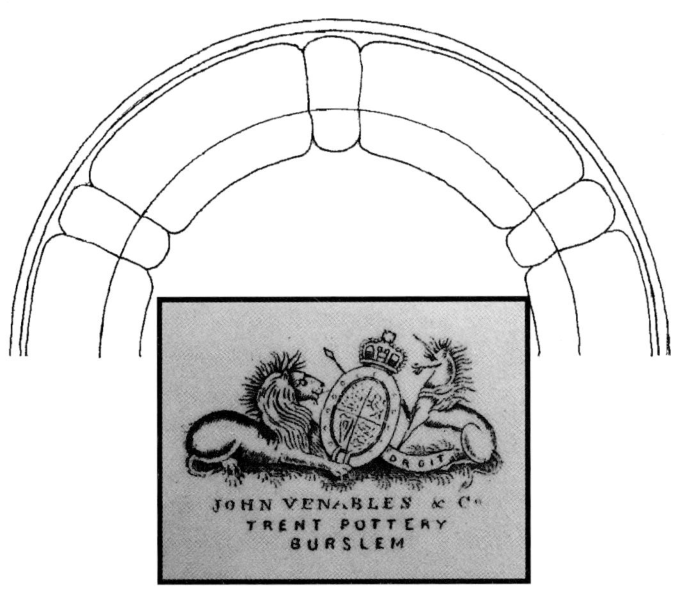

Huron Shape
(6 divisions)
William Adams, Tunstall
Reg. May 31, 1858
Skinner collection

Can be found with
Tea Leaf Lustre
Lustre Band
decoration

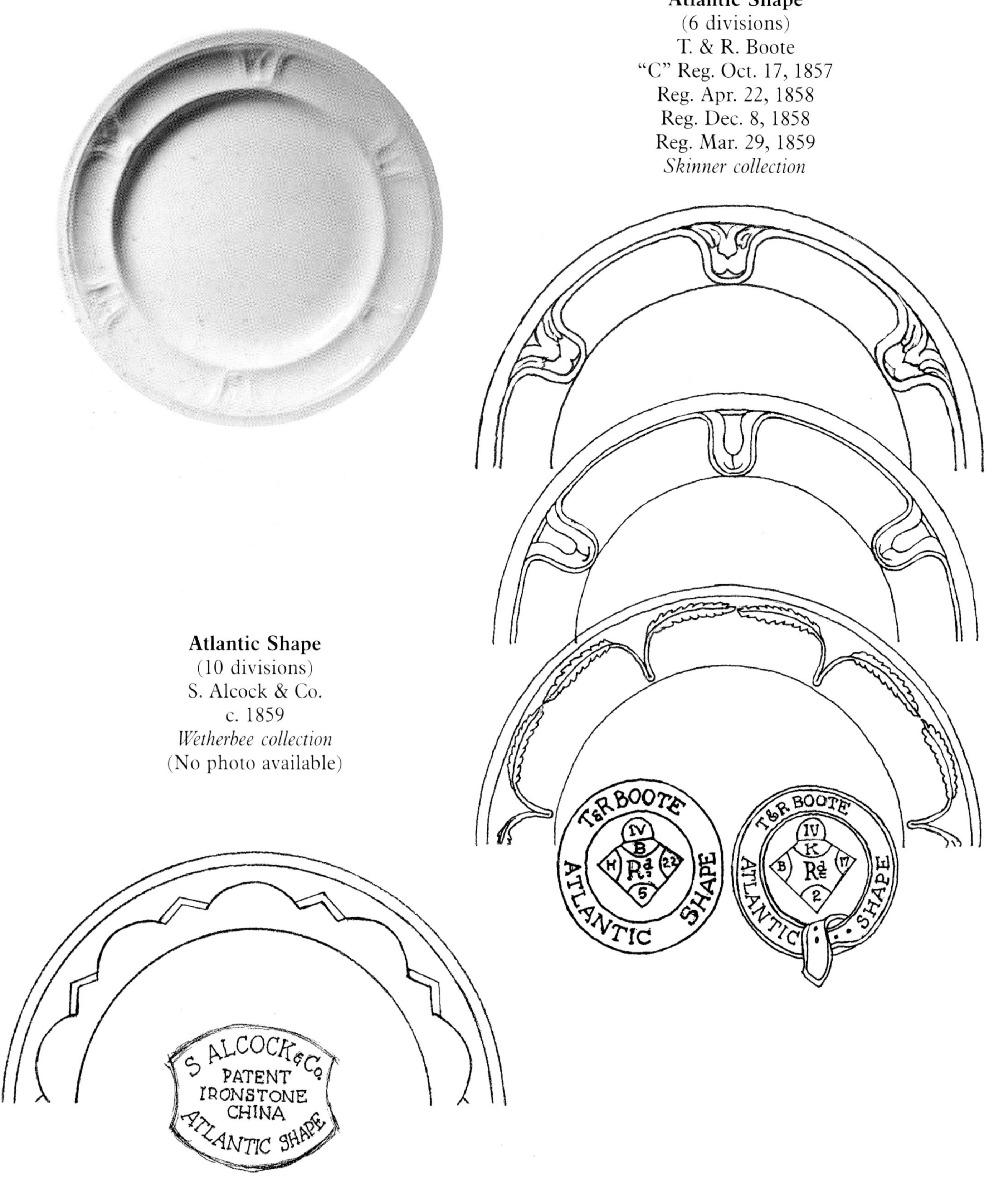

Atlantic Shape
(6 divisions)
T. & R. Boote
"C" Reg. Oct. 17, 1857
Reg. Apr. 22, 1858
Reg. Dec. 8, 1858
Reg. Mar. 29, 1859
Skinner collection

Atlantic Shape
(10 divisions)
S. Alcock & Co.
c. 1859
Wetherbee collection
(No photo available)

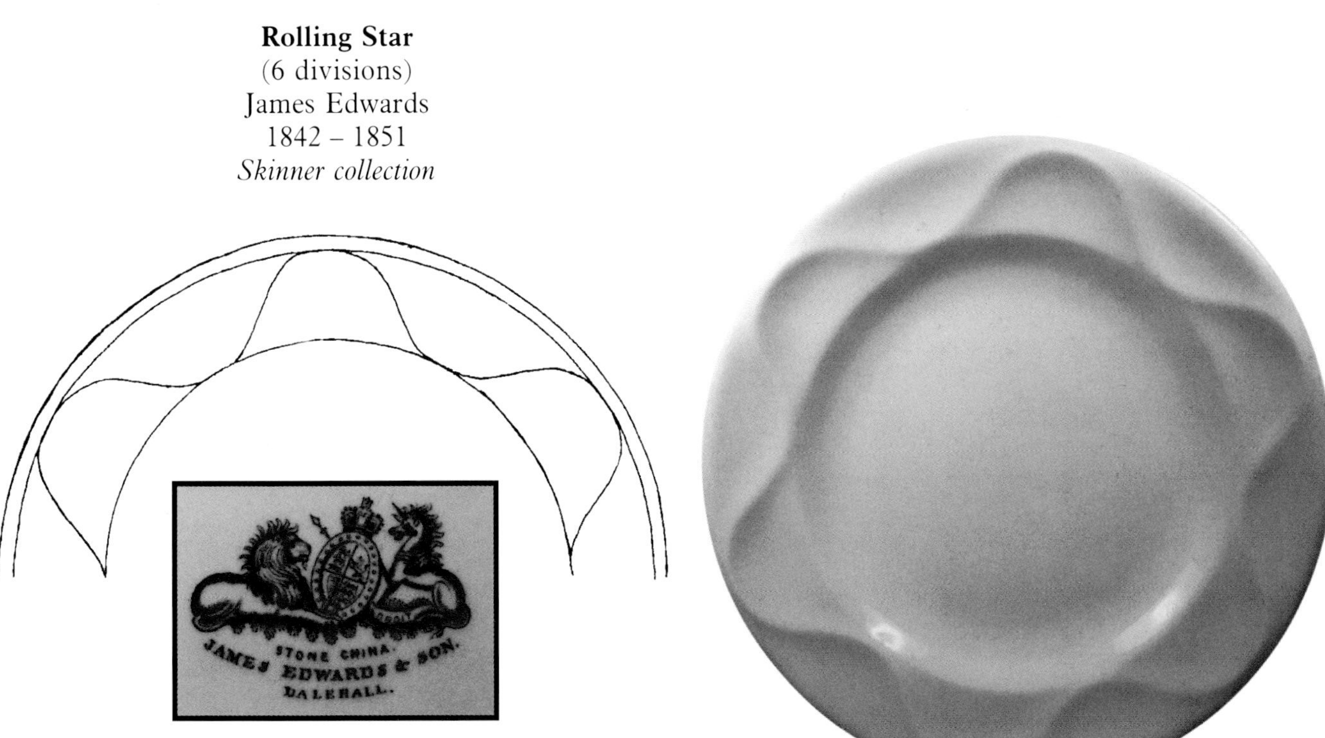

Rolling Star
(6 divisions)
James Edwards
1842 – 1851
Skinner collection

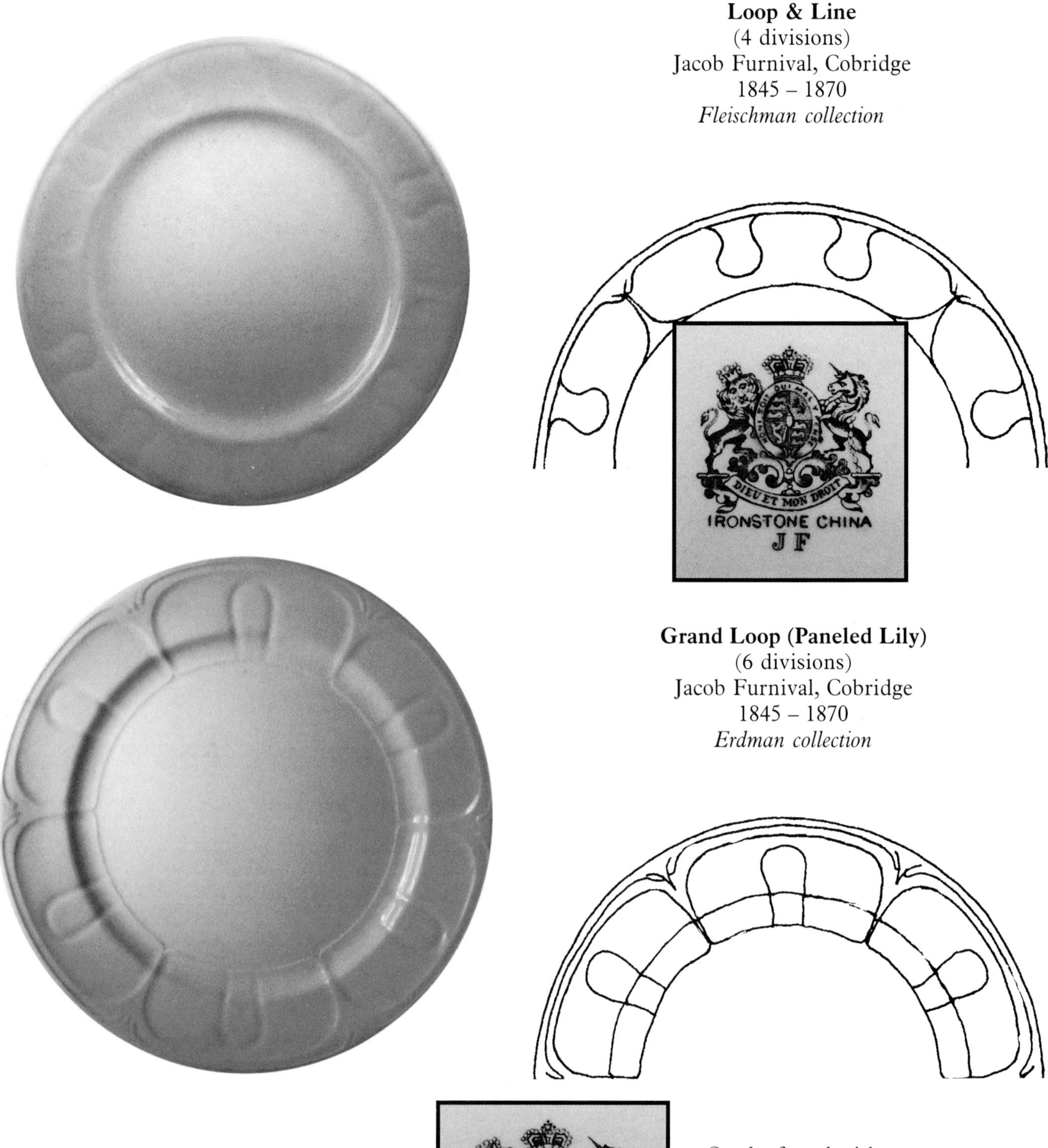

Loop & Line
(4 divisions)
Jacob Furnival, Cobridge
1845 – 1870
Fleischman collection

Grand Loop (Paneled Lily)
(6 divisions)
Jacob Furnival, Cobridge
1845 – 1870
Erdman collection

DIEU ET MON DROIT
IRONSTONE CHINA
J F

Can be found with
Teaberry Lustre
Lustre Band
Botanical Lustre
Cinquefoil Lustre
Other Lustre
decoration

Hearts

Ring 'O Hearts
(12 divisions)
Livesley & Powell
Reg. Oct. 12, 1853
Washburn collection

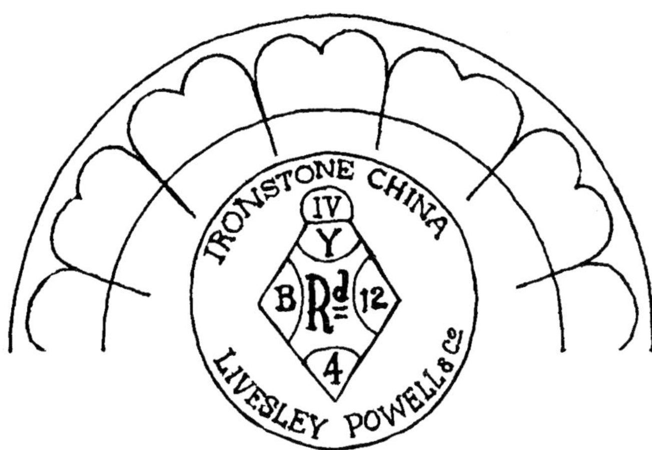

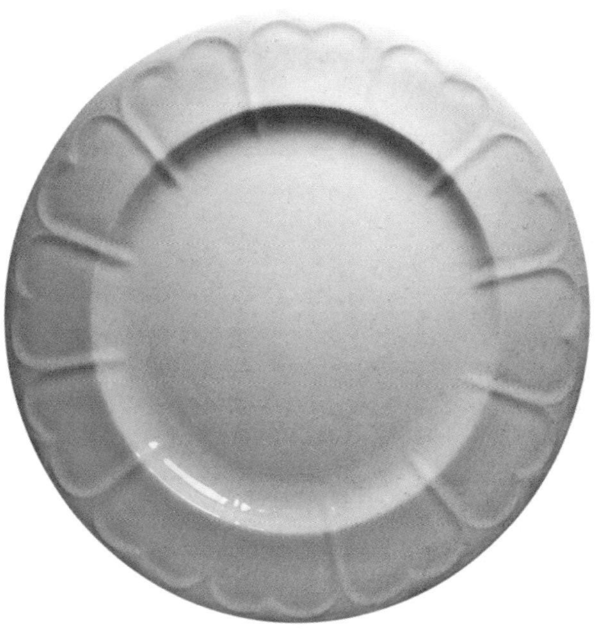

Can be found with
Teaberry Lustre
Lustre Band
Pinwheel Lustre
decoration

Adriatic Shape
(8 divisions)
Barrow & Co., Fenton
Reg. Oct. 10, 1853 and Aug. 27, 1855
Secrist collection

Ogee

President Shape
(10 divisions)
John Edwards, Fenton
Reg. Jan. 30,1855
And Jan. 5, 1856
Skinner collection

Columbia Shape
(8 divisions)
G. W. Read (Modeler)
Reg. Oct. 29, 1855
J. Clementson
Joseph Goodwin
J. Meir & Son
Livesley & Powell
Edward Challinor
E. & C. Challinor
J. & G. Meakin
G. Wooliscroft
Elsmore & Forster
W. Adams
Penman Brown & Co.
Skinner collection

Note: This registry was entered by G. W. Read, modeler of this shape. It was apparently licensed for use by many of these potters who have used the same diamond registry.

Can be found with
Lustre Band
Morning Glory Lustre
Tobacco Leaf Lustre
decoration

Boote's 1851 Round
(12 divisions)
T. & R. Boote, Burslem
Reg. July 21, 1851
Skinner collection

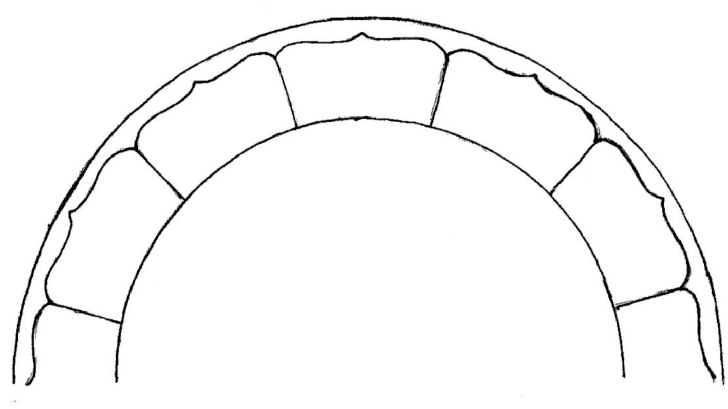

Boote's 1851 Shape
(10 sided)
T. & R. Boote, Burslem
Reg. July 21, 1851
Also Oct. 10, 1851
Skinner collection

Sydenham Shape Round
(8 divisions)
T. & R. Boote, Burslem
Reg. Sept. 3, 1853 (Y)
Also June 21, 1854 (J)
Skinner collection

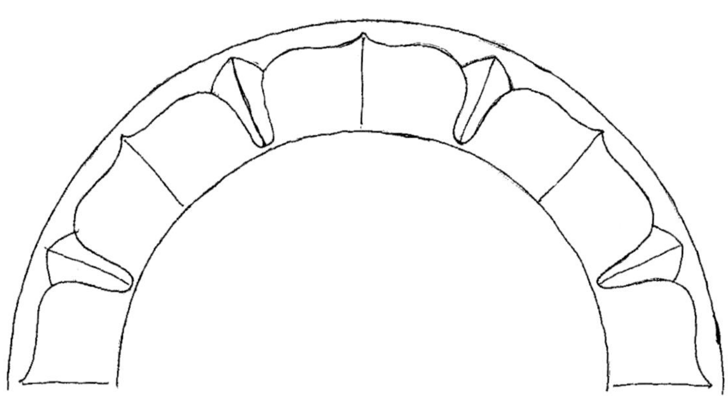

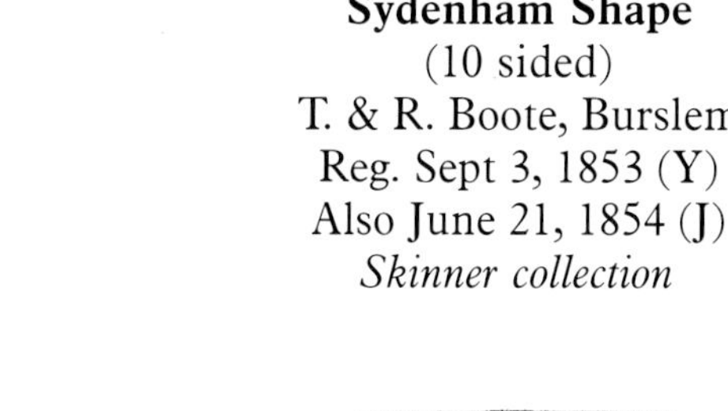

Sydenham Shape
(10 sided)
T. & R. Boote, Burslem
Reg. Sept 3, 1853 (Y)
Also June 21, 1854 (J)
Skinner collection

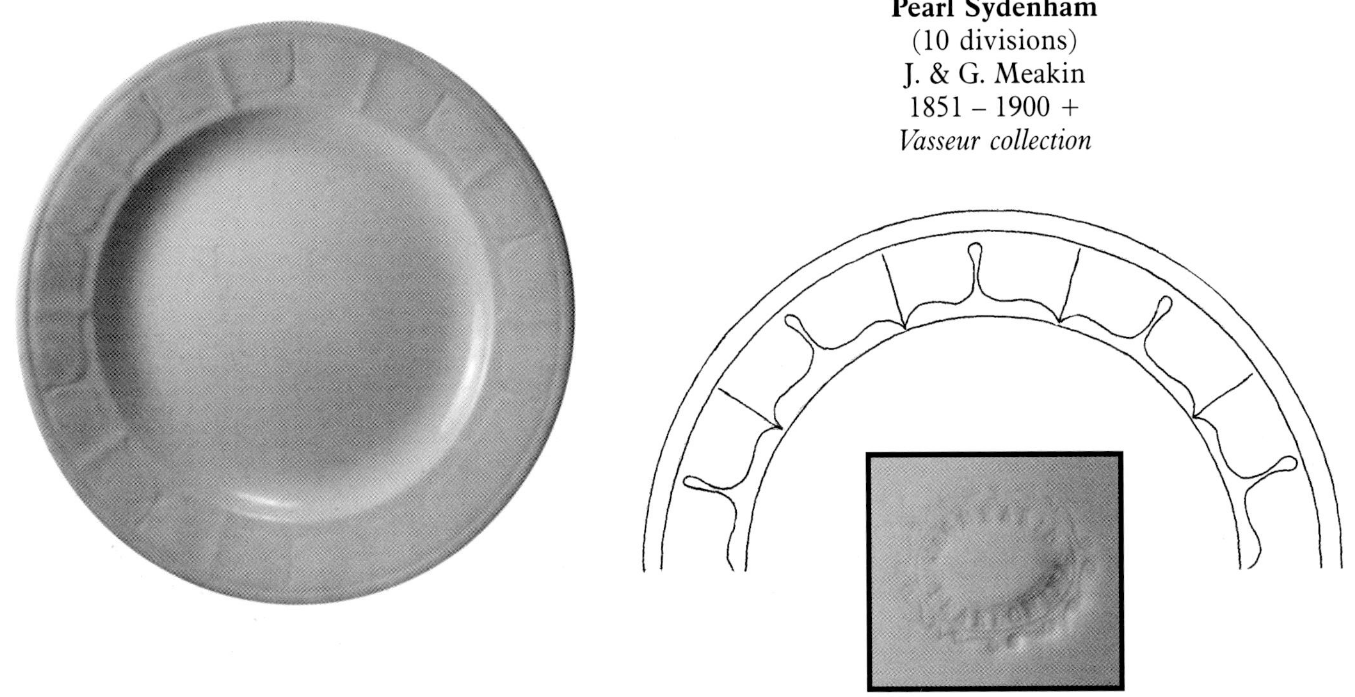

Pearl Sydenham
(10 divisions)
J. & G. Meakin
1851 – 1900 +
Vasseur collection

Pearson's No. 5 Shape
(8 divisions)
E. Pearson, Cobridge
1850 – 1873
Skinner collection
Persia Shape
E. Corn, Burslem
1853 – 1864
Yunginger collection
also known as
Pearl Sydenham #2
J. & G. Meakin, Hanley
1851 – 1900 +
Another example of a shape that was probably registered by a modeler.

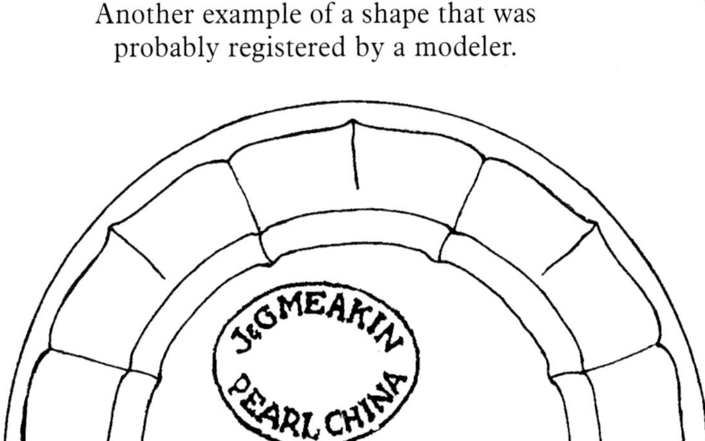

Havelock Shape
(8 inverted divisions)
Holland & Green
Reg. May 31, 1858 #113900
Stocki collection

Panelled Grape
(8 everted divisions)
Jacob Furnival
1845 – 1870
Joseph Clementson
1839 – 1864
Oliver collection
Clementson's Paneled Grape plate may be different. No photo available.

Can be found with
Teaberry Lustre
Lustre Band
Botanical Lustre
Cinquefoil Lustre
Pinwheel Lustre
Other Lustre decoration

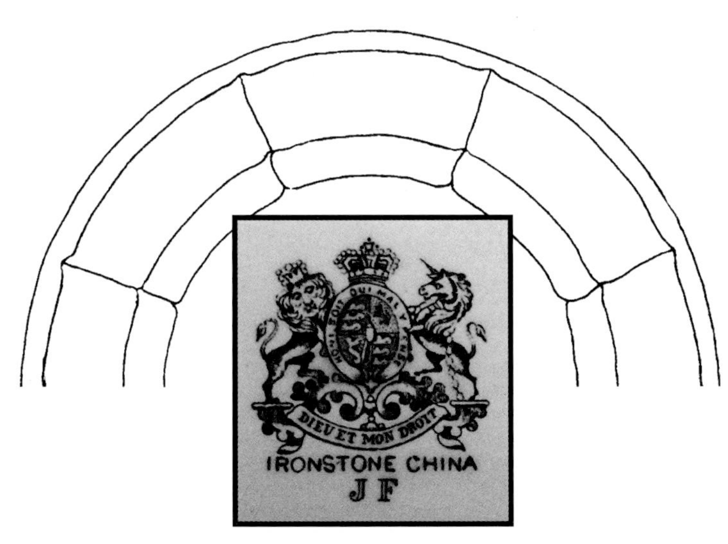

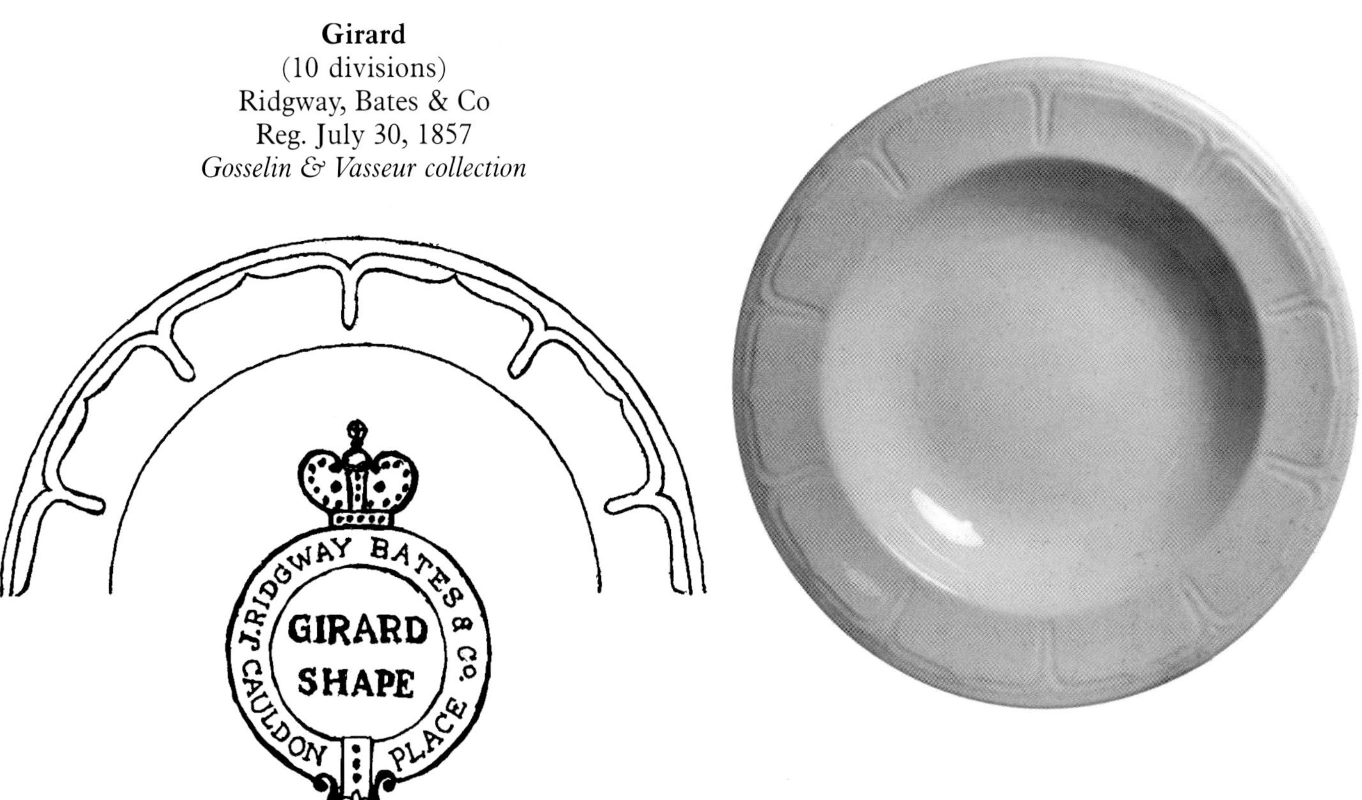

Girard
(10 divisions)
Ridgway, Bates & Co
Reg. July 30, 1857
Gosselin & Vasseur collection

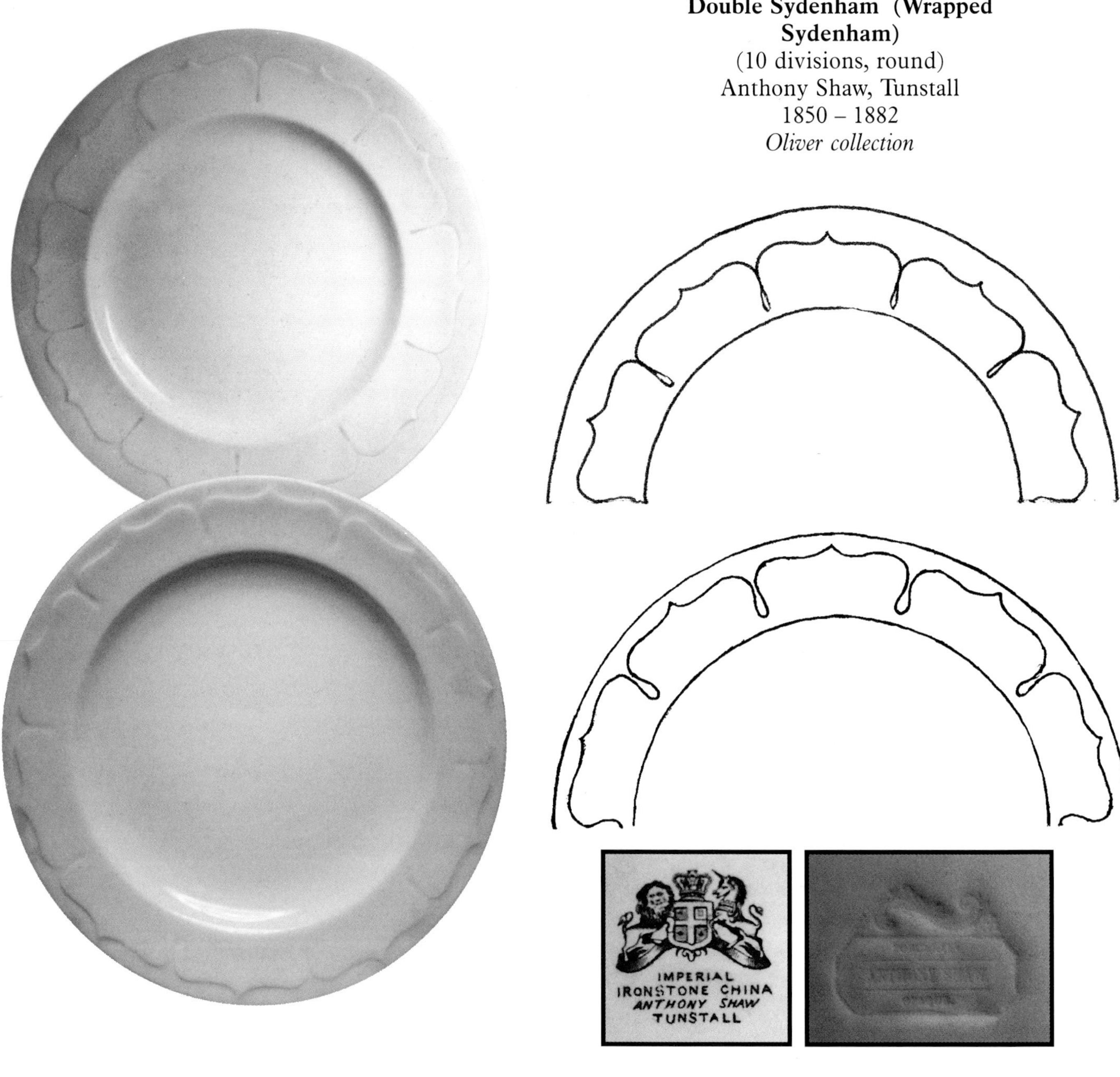

Double Sydenham (Wrapped Sydenham)
(10 divisions, round)
Anthony Shaw, Tunstall
1850 – 1882
Oliver collection

Can be found with
Tea Leaf Lustre
Pre-Tea Leaf Lustre
Lustre Band
Scallop
Other Lustre
decoration

Double Sydenham (Wrapped Sydenham)
(10 divisions, sided)
T. Goodfellow
E. Walley
W. Adams
Holland & Green
S. Hughes & Son
W. & E. Corn
John Maddock
Livesley & Powell
This shape was probably registered by a modeler in the 1850s.
Cora Shape
John Alcock
Skinner collection

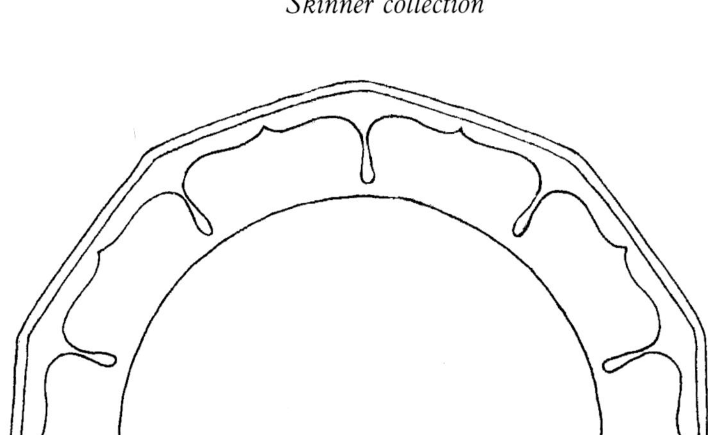

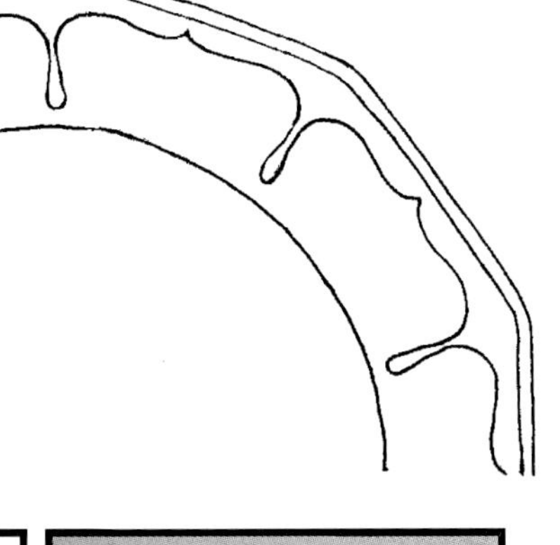

Can be found with
Tea Leaf Lustre
Pre-Tea Leaf Lustre
Lustre Band
Scallop
Other Lustre
decoration

Baltic Shape
(10 sided and 10 divisions)
Reg. Oct. 25, 1855 by D Chetwynd (Modeler)
J. Meir & Son, Cobridge
T. Hulme
G. Wooliscroft
Mississippi Shape
E. Pearson
Maltese Shape
E. Corn
Dallas Shape
J. Clementson
Skinner collection
Can be found with
Lustre Band
decoration

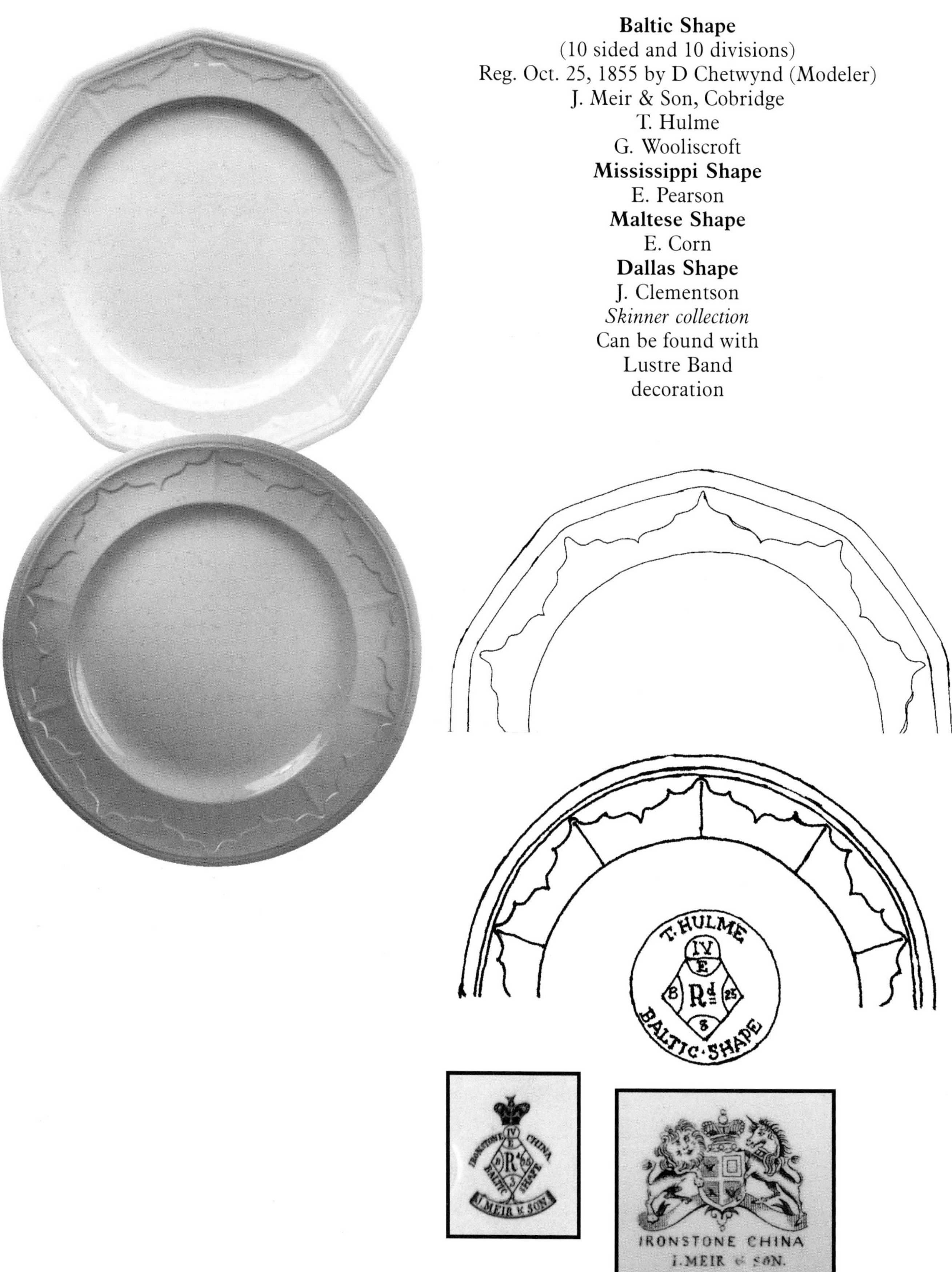

Ogee and Scallop

Scalloped Decagon/Cambridge Shape
(10 sided and round with 6 divisions)
J. Wedgwood or Davenport, Longport
Reg. Oct. 23, 1852 also Jan. 14, 1853
Reg. Oct. 6, 1854 by Davenport
Skinner collection

Scalloped Decagon is the popular name but this shape was registered as Cambridge Shape.
Wedgwood and Davenport, who were related by marriage, shared the registry marks.

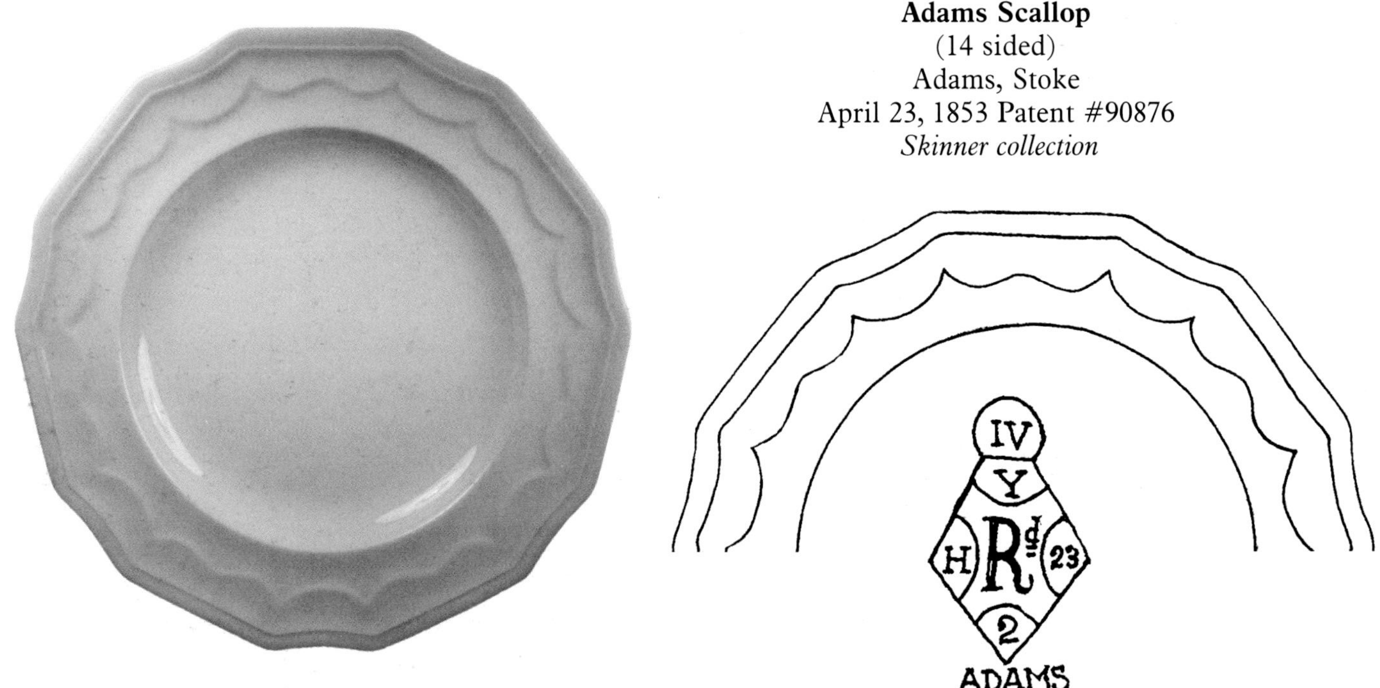

Adams Scallop
(14 sided)
Adams, Stoke
April 23, 1853 Patent #90876
Skinner collection

Hebe Shape (Goddess of Youth)
(5 divisions)
John Alcock, Cobridge
Reg. May 7, 1853
Dieringer collection

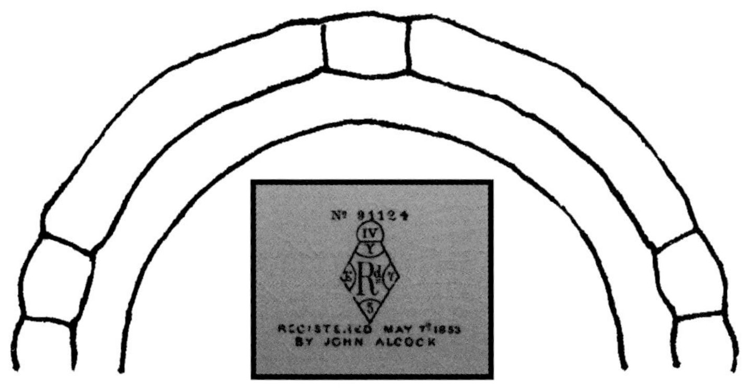

Wooliscroft Gothic
(4 divisions)
G. Wooliscroft
Reg. Feb. 10, 1853
Erdman collection

Scroll and Swirl

Prize Puritan
(4 divisions)
T. J. & J. Mayer, Longport
Reg. Sept. 2, 1851
This is the shape that was registered the year the prize was awarded.
Wetherbee collection

Prize Bloom
(10 sided)
T. J. & J. Mayer, Longport
Reg. Oct. 22, 1853
The 1851 Prize Medal mark was used for sales purposes on this 1853 Shape.
Moreland collection

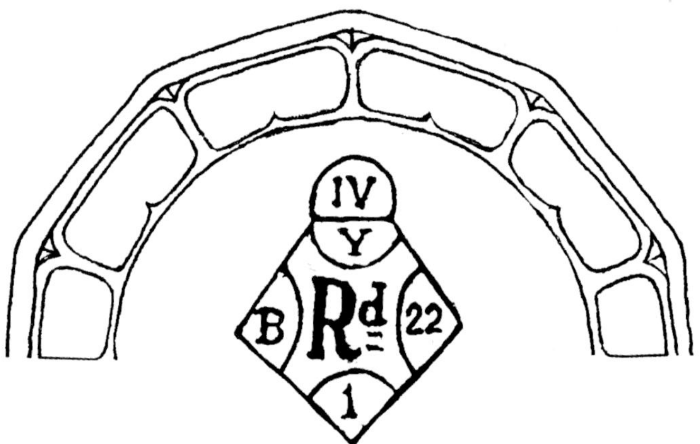

St. Louis Shape
(4 divisions)
J. Edwards, Fenton
c. 1853
Volckening collection

Alcock's Unnamed
(5 divisions)
J. & G. Alcock, Cobridge
1839 – 1846
Noble collection

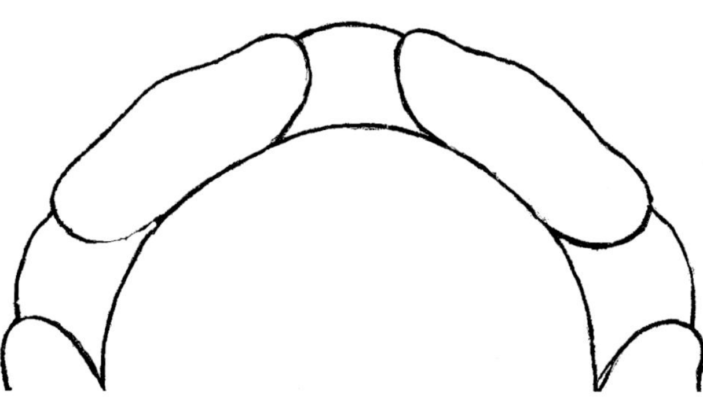

Berlin Swirl
(5 divisions)
T. J. & J. Mayer
Reg. Jan. 21, 1845
Mayer & Elliot
Reg. Dec. 18, 1856
Liddle Elliot & Son
1864
Skinner collection

Although most of the dinner set has been found in round and oval shape, a 10-sided cup plate (photo top left) and an octagonal platter have been seen.
Mattice collection

Hanging Arch
(8 divisions)
James Edwards & Son, Dale Hall
1852 – 1881
Skinner collection

Scrolled Bubble
(8 divisions)
J. W. Pankhurst, Hanley
1850 – 1851
Skinner collection

Hill Shape (Medallion Scroll)
(4 divisions)
Clementson, Hanley
Reg. Oct. 19, 1860
Erdman collection

Can be found with
Teaberry Lustre
Lustre Band
Coral Lustre
decoration

Ribbed

Full Ribbed (Ribbed Raspberry)
J. W. Pankhurst, Hanley
c. 1855
Lautenschlager collection

Ribbed Fern
(6 divisions)
A. J. Wilkinson
(No photo available)

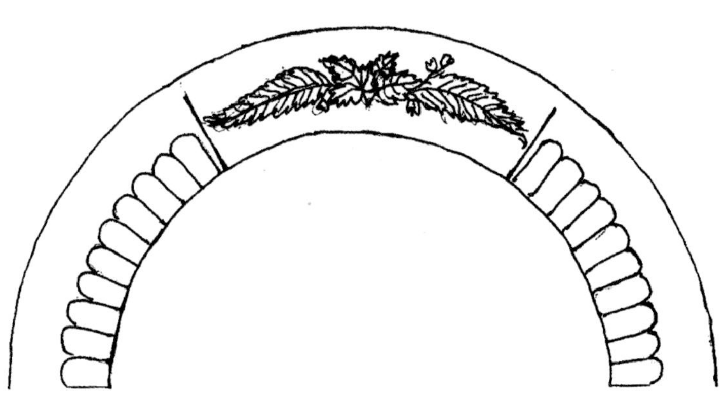

Ribbed Raspberry with Bloom
J. & G. Meakin, Hanley
c. 1860
Dieringer collection

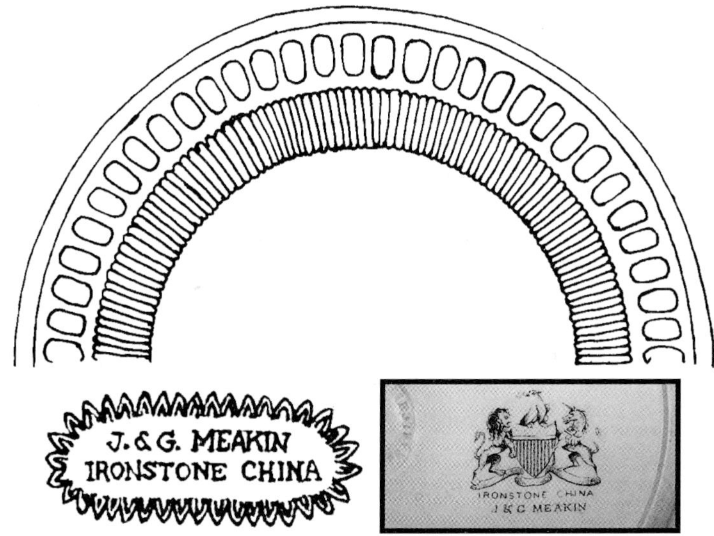

Ribbed Chain
J. W. Pankhurst
c. 1860
Erdman collection

J.F.'s Dover Shape
Jacob Furnival
Reg. April 30, 1845
Gortzig collection

Dover Shape
(14 divisions)
W. Adams, Tunstall
Reg. Mar. 13, 1862
Erdman collection

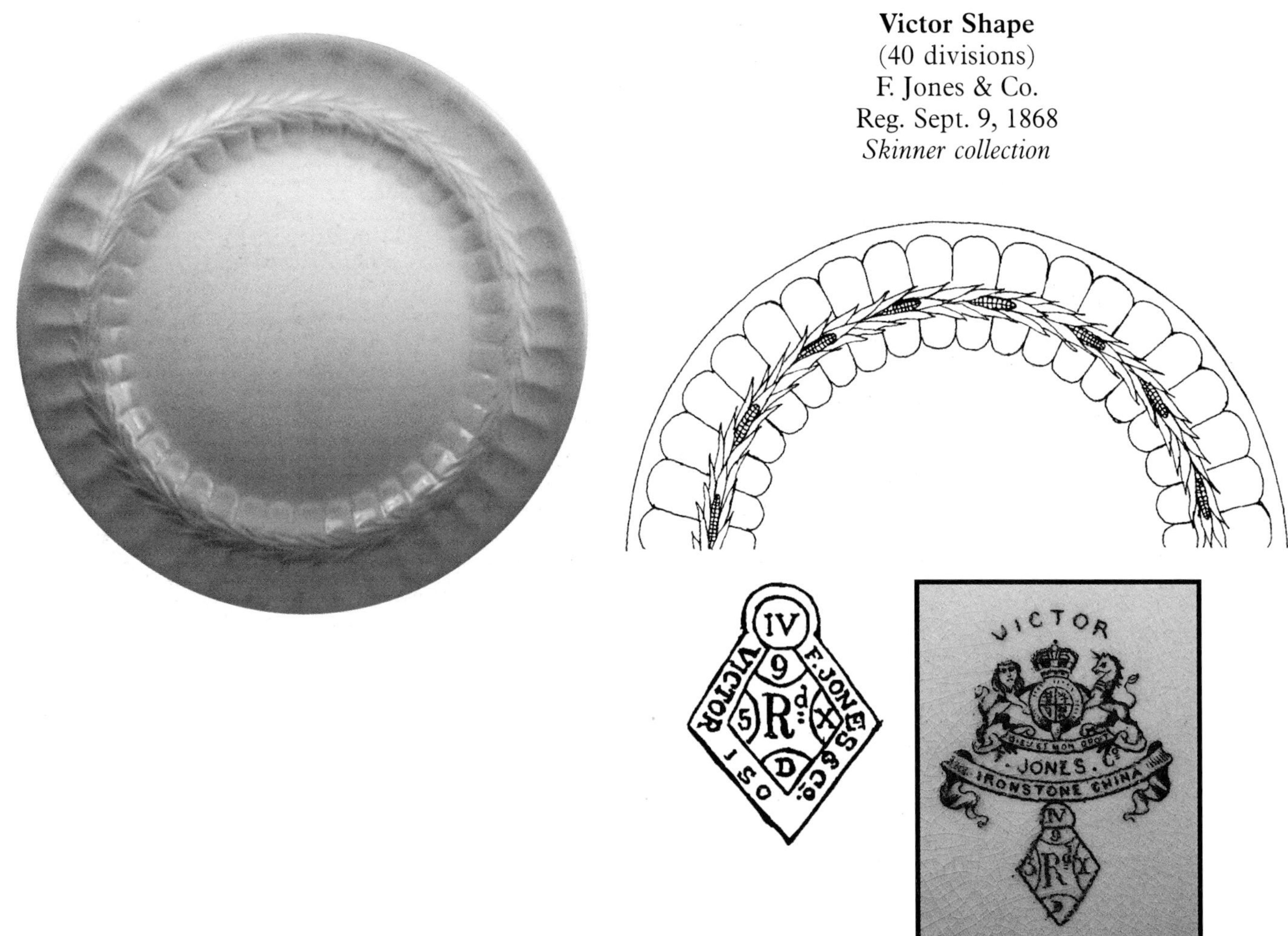

Victor Shape
(40 divisions)
F. Jones & Co.
Reg. Sept. 9, 1868
Skinner collection

Laurel Wreath Shape (Victory Shape)
(40 divisions)
Elsmore & Forster
Reg. April 4, 1867
(Note: registered two different names on the same day.)
Skinner collection

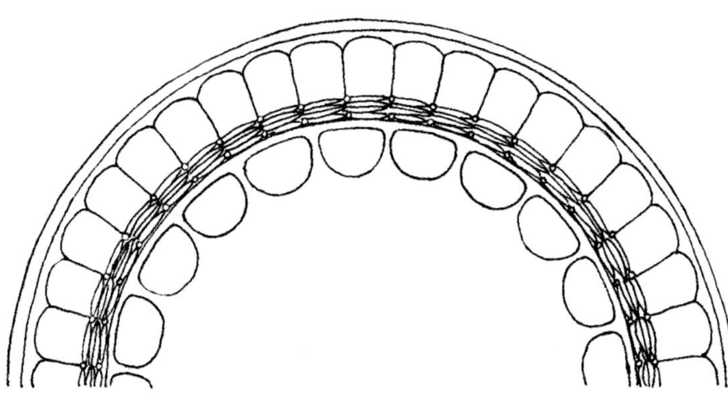

Can be found with
Other Lustre
decoration

Luster enhancement of
embossed details.

Eagle (Diamond Thumbprint)
(30 divisions)
Gelson Bros., Hanley
Reg. April 14, 1866
Rich collection

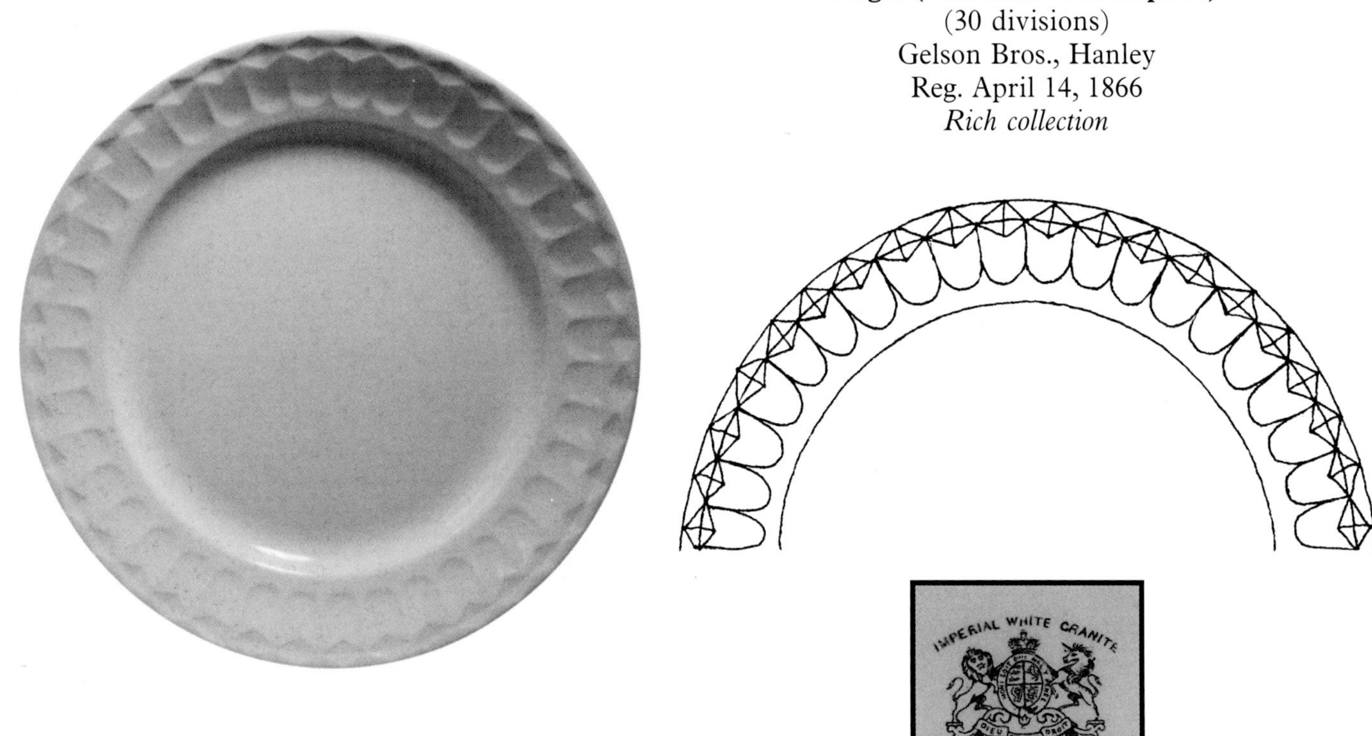

Nile Shape
(30 divisions)
George L. Ashworth & Bros., Hanley
Reg. April 14, 1866
Rich collection

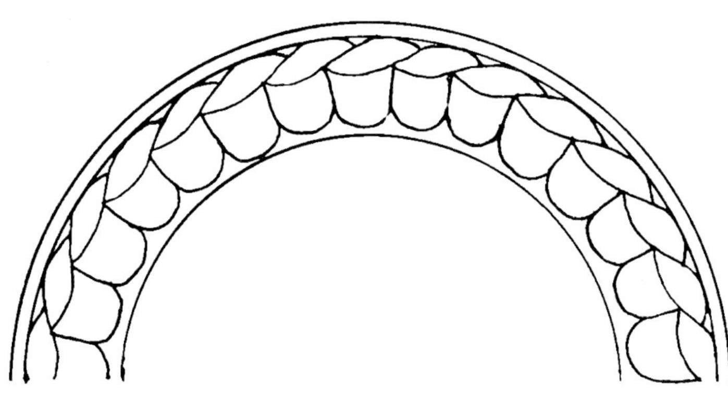

Classical

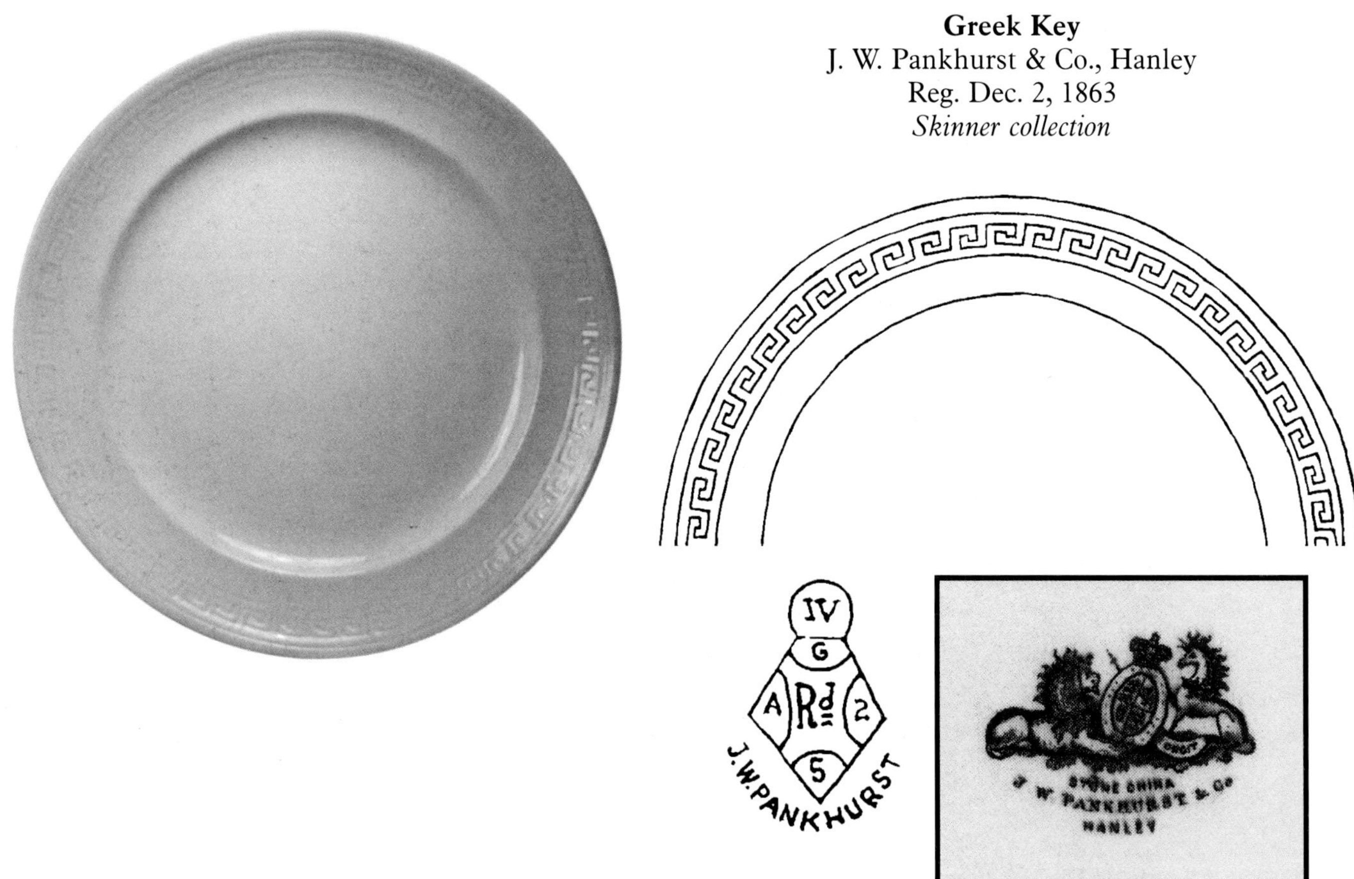

Greek Key
J. W. Pankhurst & Co., Hanley
Reg. Dec. 2, 1863
Skinner collection

Olympic Shape
Elsmore & Forster, Tunstall
Reg. Nov. 10, 1864
Washburn collection

Athena Shape
(5 divisions)
Reg. Sept 11, 1865
Thos. Cooper (exer. of)
Skinner collection

Athenia Shape
(5 divisions)
J. T. Close & Co., Stoke Upon Trent
Reg. Jan. 3, 1866 No. 194194
W. Adams & Son, Stoke
Skinner collection

Leaf

Framed Leaf
(8 sided)
Samuel Alcock & Co./Colbridge
c. 1849-51
Skinner collection

Framed Leaf
(6 divisions)
J. W. Pankhurst / Hanley
c. 1850
Skinner collection

Leaf Focus
(5 divisions)
Taylor Bros., Hanley
c. 1869-1875
Skinner collection

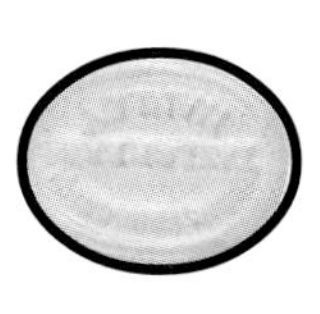

FPO Photo 10a/5 (use both images)
outline and box-bfi

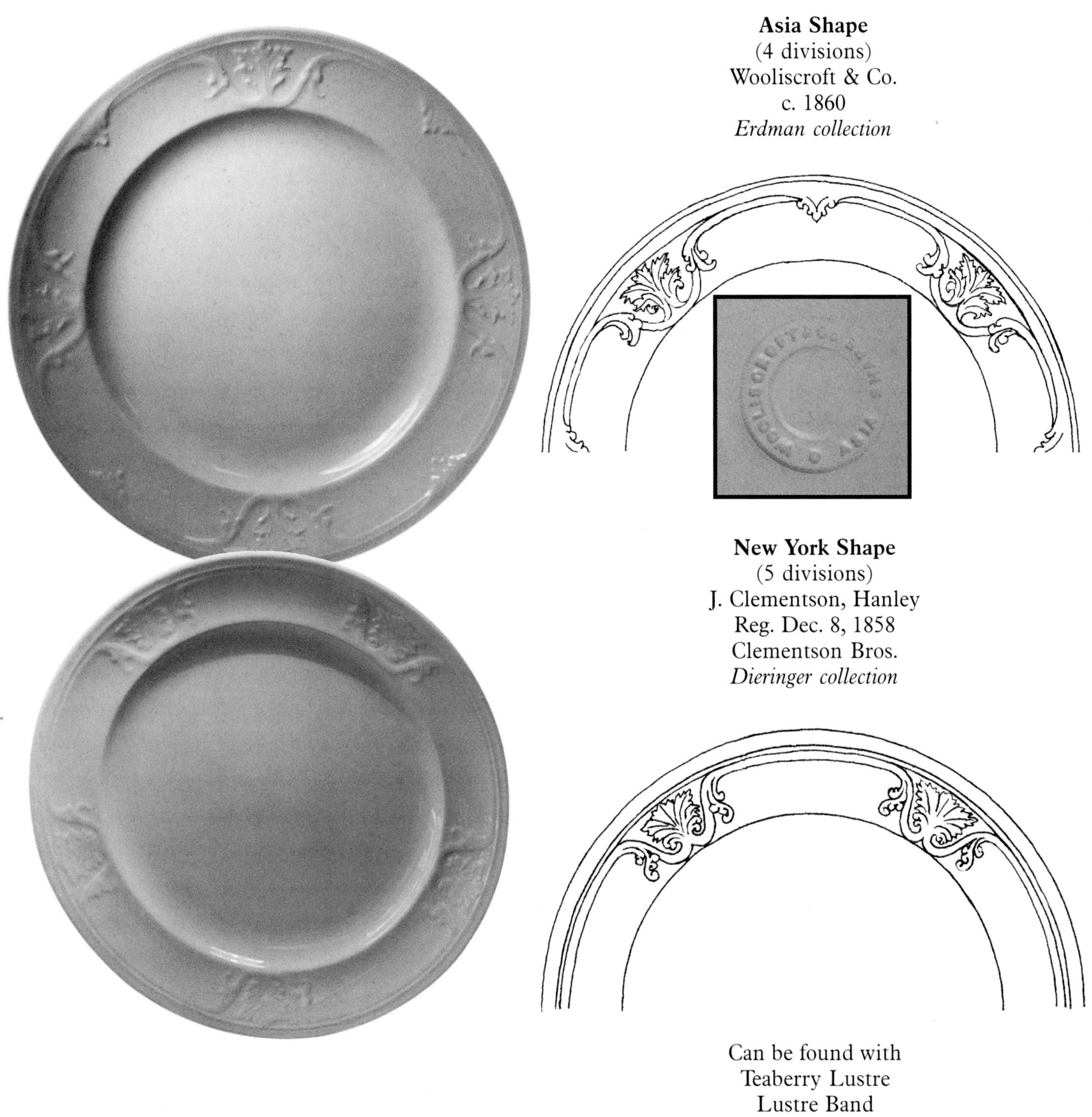

Asia Shape
(4 divisions)
Wooliscroft & Co.
c. 1860
Erdman collection

New York Shape
(5 divisions)
J. Clementson, Hanley
Reg. Dec. 8, 1858
Clementson Bros.
Dieringer collection

Can be found with
Teaberry Lustre
Lustre Band
Coral Lustre
Other Lustre decoration

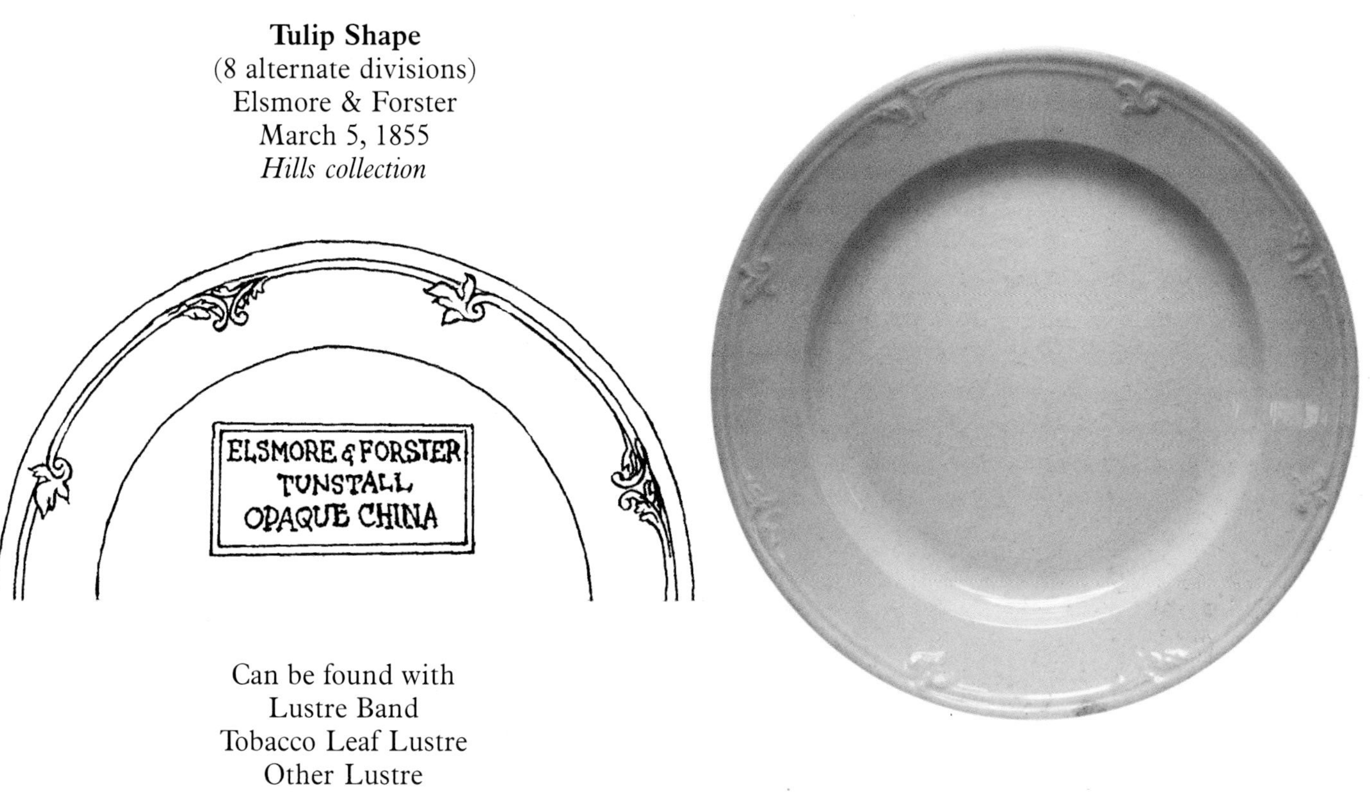

Tulip Shape
(8 alternate divisions)
Elsmore & Forster
March 5, 1855
Hills collection

Can be found with
Lustre Band
Tobacco Leaf Lustre
Other Lustre
decoration

Twin Leaves
(16-sided, 8 divisions)
James Edwards / Dalehall
Reg. Sept. 29, 1851 # M80816
Hills collection

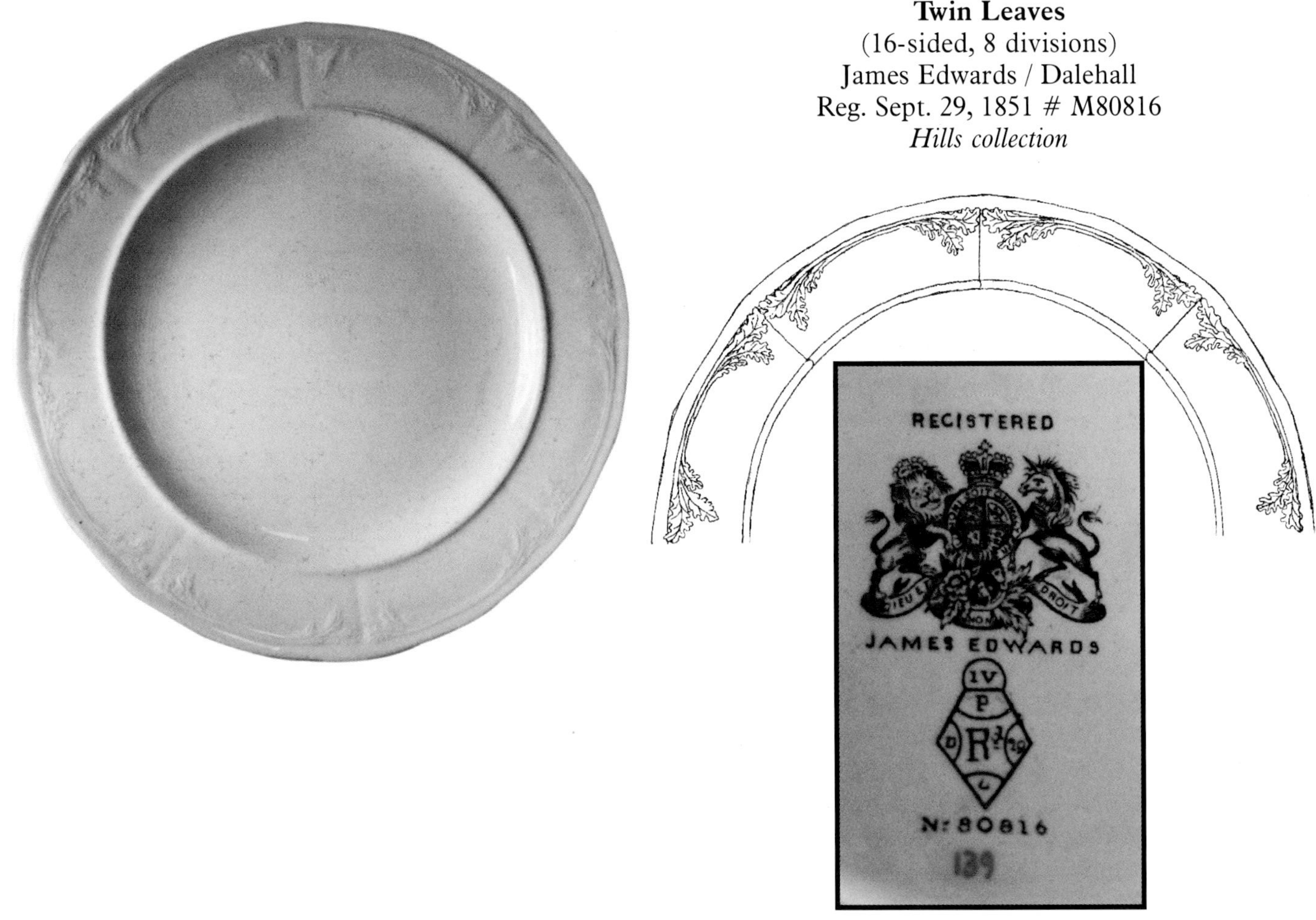

Tuscan Shape
(8 divisions)
Sometimes marked President Shape
by potter's error.
John Edwards, Longton
Reg. July 18, 1853
Hills collection

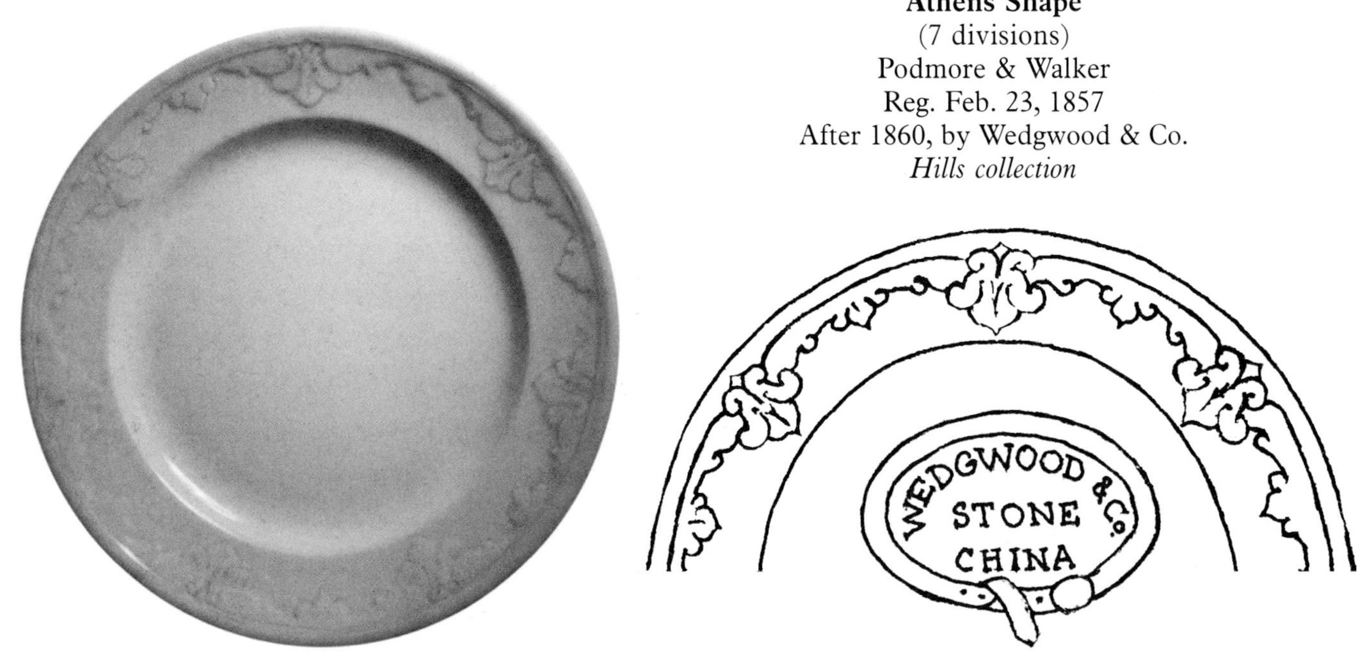

Athens Shape
(7 divisions)
Podmore & Walker
Reg. Feb. 23, 1857
After 1860, by Wedgwood & Co.
Hills collection

Acorn

Tiny Oak & Acorn
(8 divisions)
J. W. Pankhurst, Hanley
c. 1860s
Skinner collection

Round Acorn
(5 divisions)
Baker & Chetwynd, Burslem
c. late 1860s
Erdman collection

BAKER & CHETWYND
BURSLEM
IRONSTONE CHINA

Fruit and Vine

Balanced Vine
Clementson Bros., Hanley
Reg. May 22, 1867
Miller collection

Can be found with
Teaberry Lustre
Lustre Band
decoration

Fig/Union Shape
J. Wedgwood, Tunstall
Davenport, Longport
Dinner service Reg. Nov. 14, 1856
Tea and Toiletware Reg. Nov. 27, 1856
Skinner collection

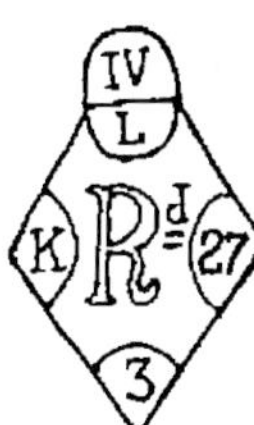

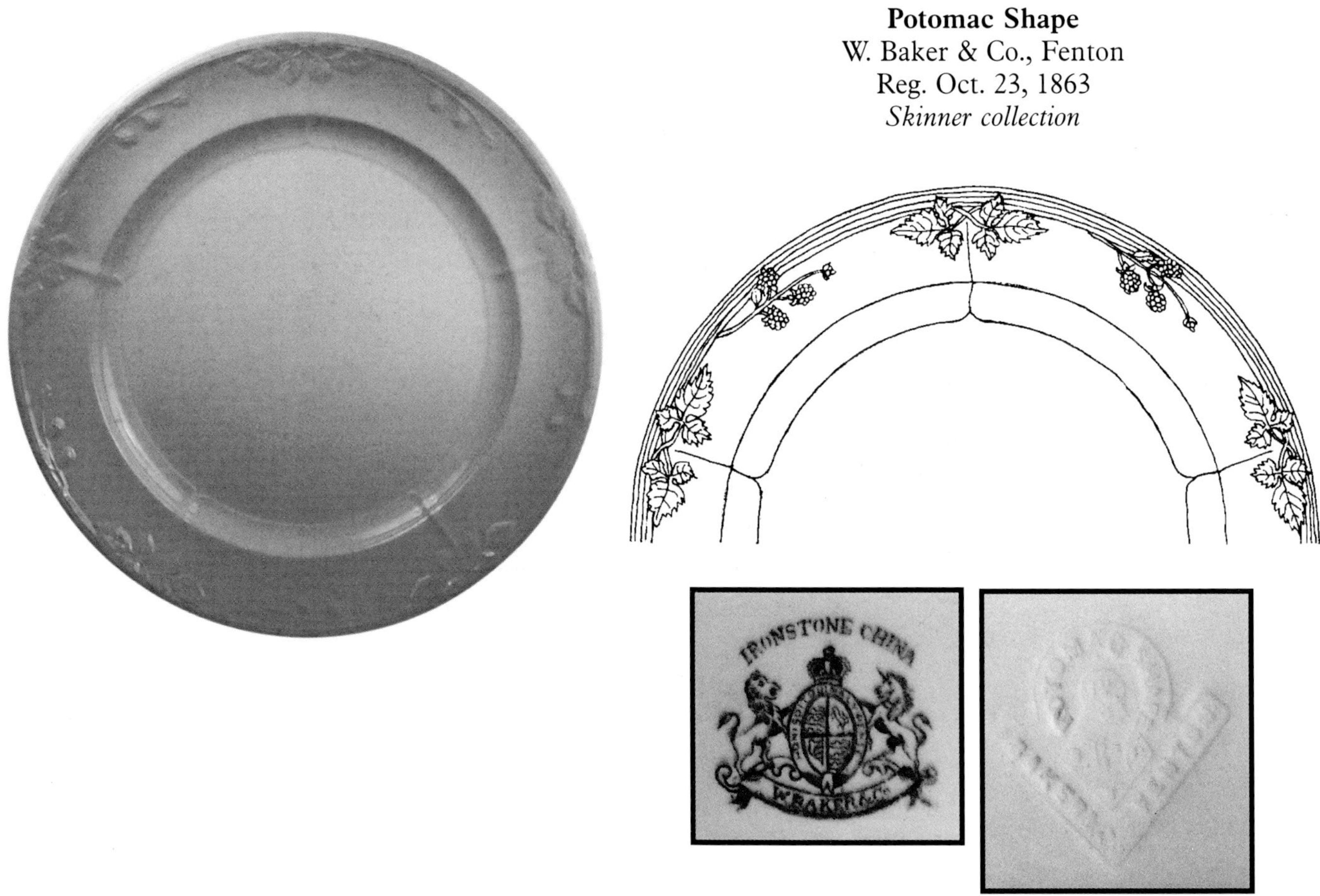

Potomac Shape
W. Baker & Co., Fenton
Reg. Oct. 23, 1863
Skinner collection

Vine

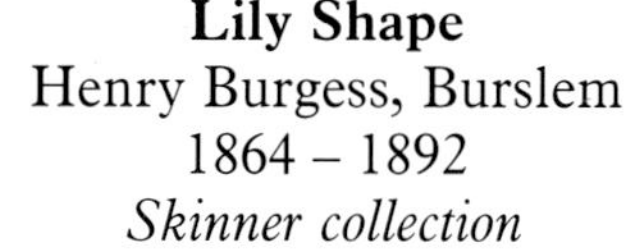

Lily Shape
Henry Burgess, Burslem
1864 – 1892
Skinner collection

Morning Glory (Halleck Shape)
Elsmore & Forster
1853-1871
Moreland collection

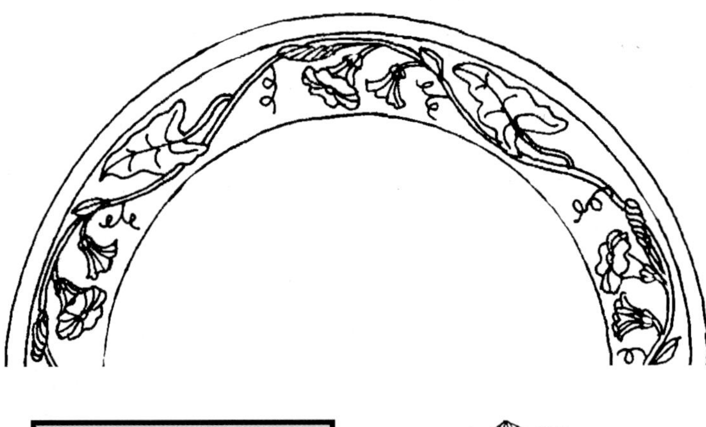

Morning Glory
(5 divisions)
James Edwards & Son, Dale Hall
Reg. March 21, 1863
(No photo available)

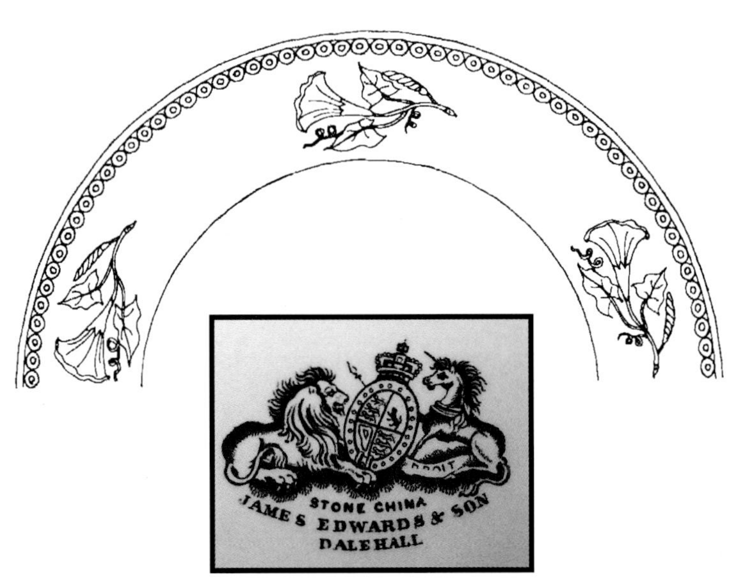

Ivy Wreath
John Meir & Son
Reg. May 2, 1860
Kerr collectoion

Wreath of Leaves
Unknown maker (Possibly Jacob Furnival, the mark is similar)
Lautenschlager collection

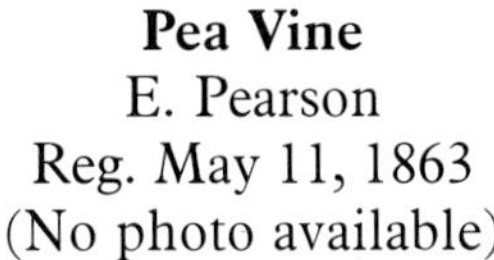

Pea Vine
E. Pearson
Reg. May 11, 1863
(No photo available)

Vine with Coral Bells
Moore Brothers, Cobridge
Cambridge (Possibly another named shape)
Reg. Nov. 17, 1868 #224389
Washburn collection

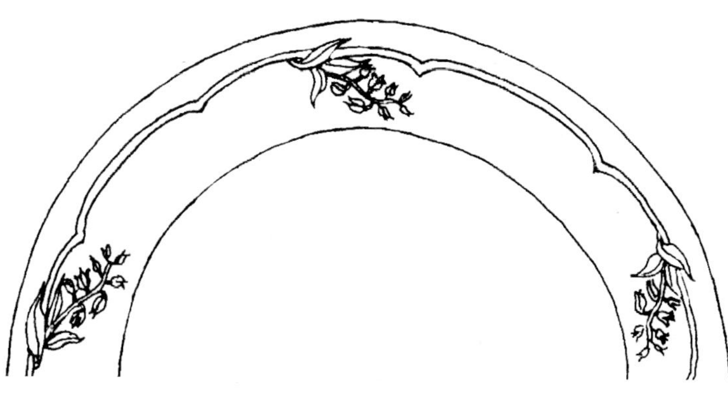

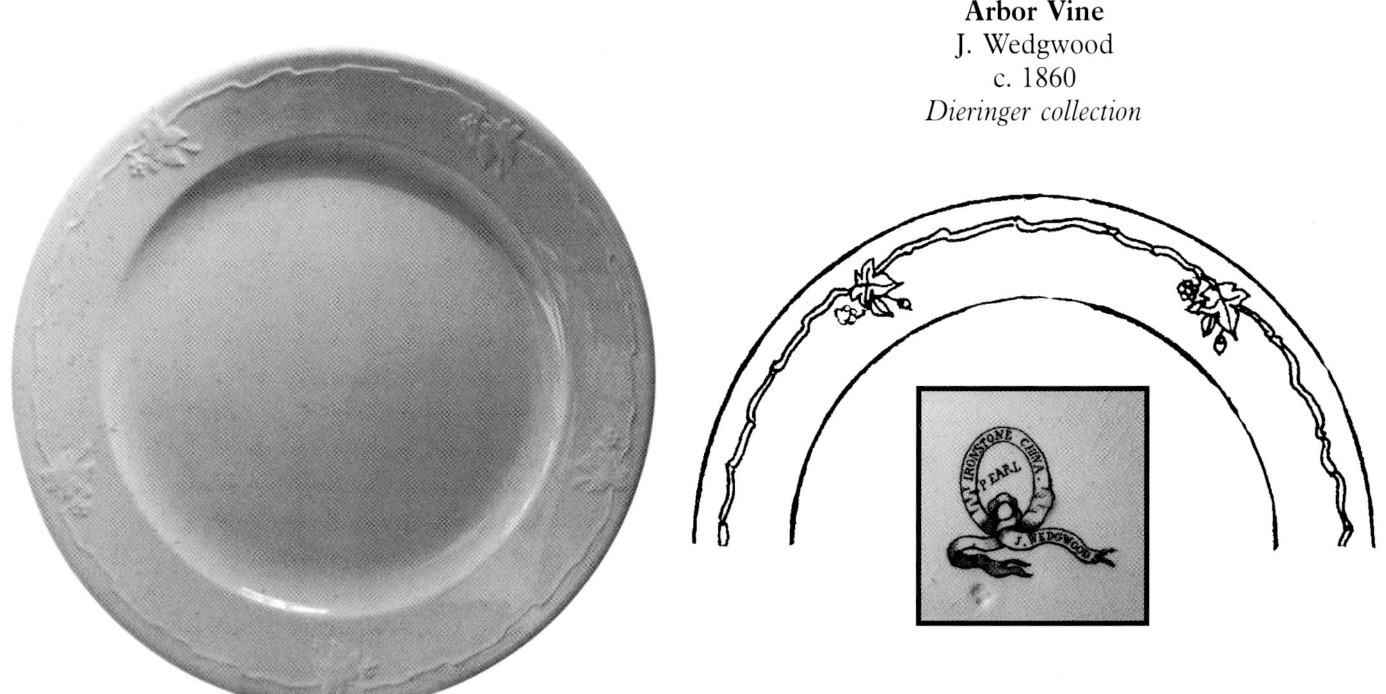

Arbor Vine
J. Wedgwood
c. 1860
Dieringer collection

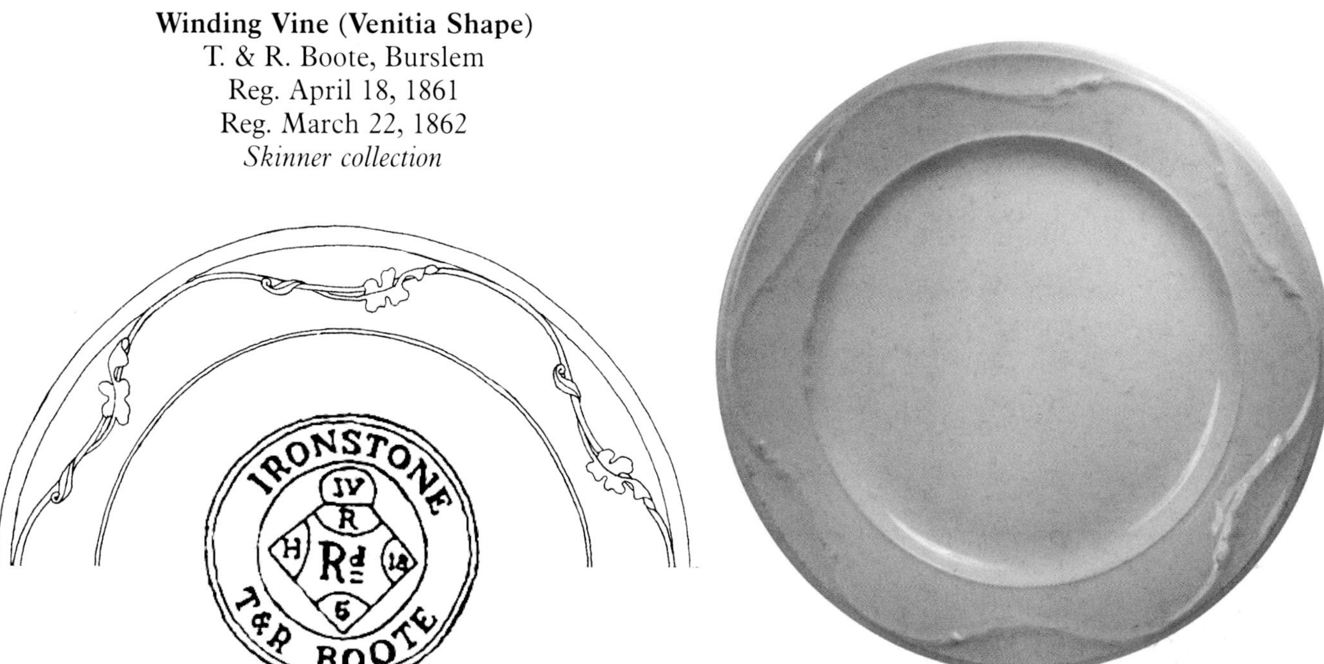

Winding Vine (Venitia Shape)
T. & R. Boote, Burslem
Reg. April 18, 1861
Reg. March 22, 1862
Skinner collection

Laurel Shape
Wedgwood & Co.
After 1860
Skinner collection

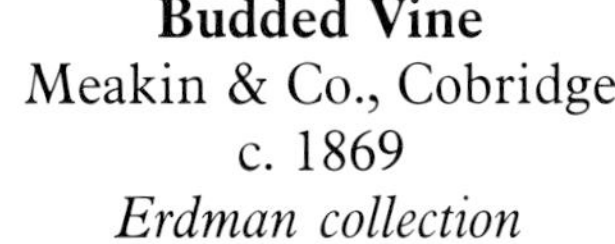

Budded Vine
Meakin & Co., Cobridge
c. 1869
Erdman collection

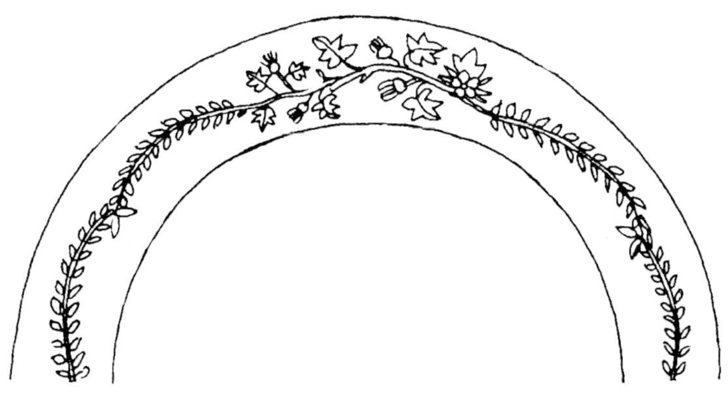

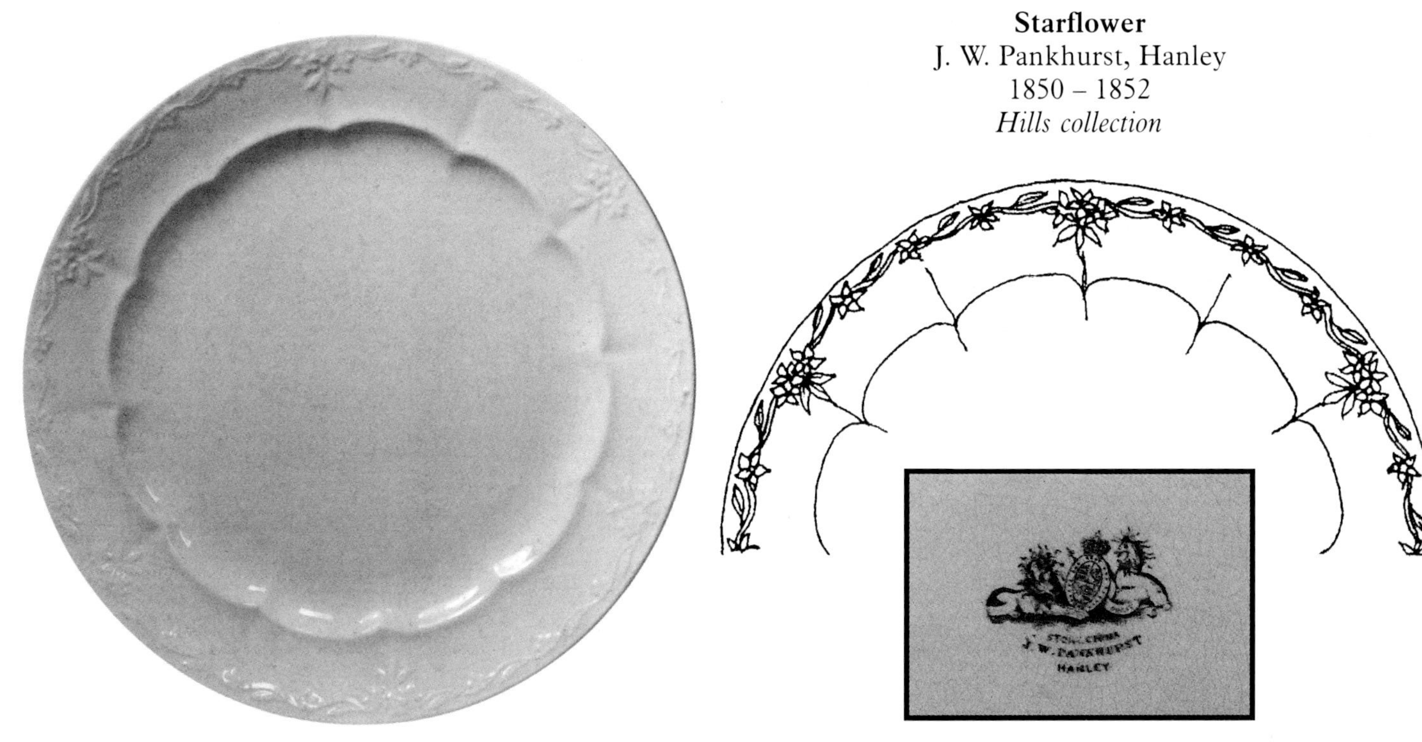

Starflower
J. W. Pankhurst, Hanley
1850 – 1852
Hills collection

Bordered Gooseberry
Wedgwood & Co.
c. 1860
Hills collection

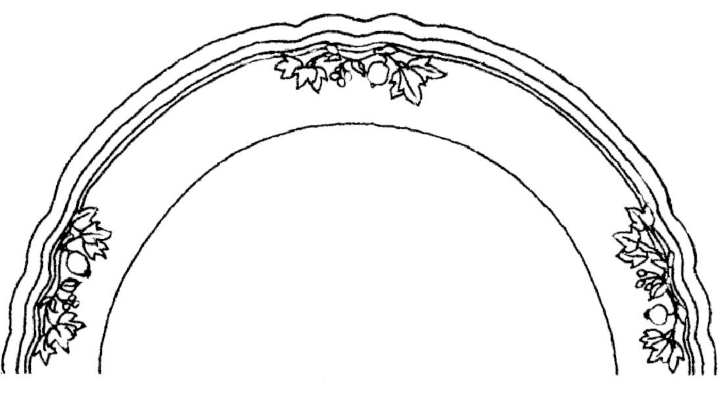

Flora (two versions)
Wedgwood & Co.
c. 1860
Skinner collection

Bell-Shaped Flowers

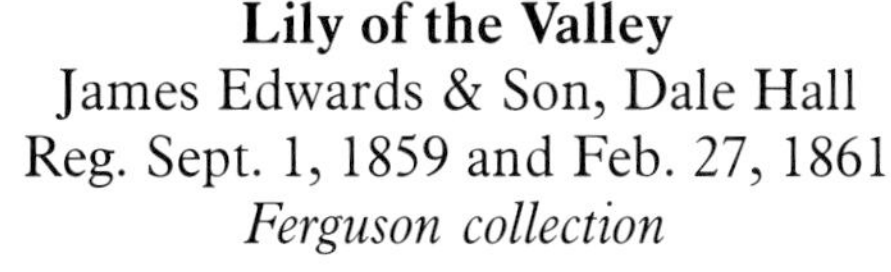

Lily of the Valley
James Edwards & Son, Dale Hall
Reg. Sept. 1, 1859 and Feb. 27, 1861
Ferguson collection

Lily of the Valley
Anthony Shaw
1856 – 1882
Ferguson collection

Can be found with
Tea Leaf Lustre
Lustre Band
decoration

Lily of the Valley with Thumbprint
J.F.
1845 – 1870
Skinner collection

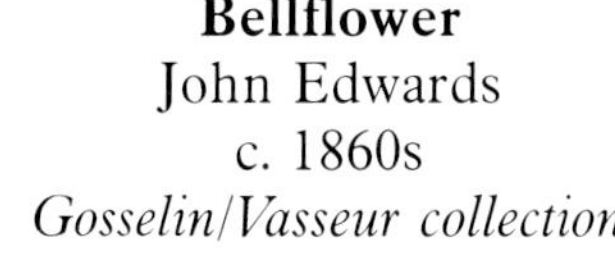

Bellflower
John Edwards
c. 1860s
Gosselin/Vasseur collection

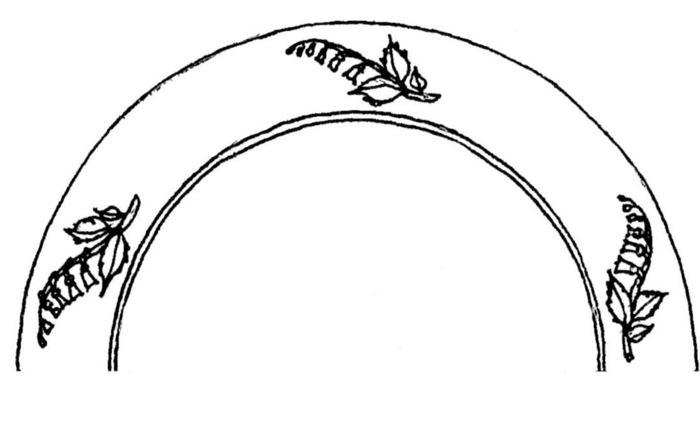

Cochran's Ring (Hyacinth)
R. Cochran & Co., Glasgow
1856-1896
Abrams collection

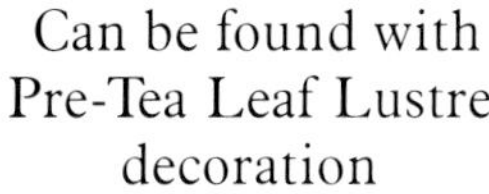

Can be found with
Pre-Tea Leaf Lustre
decoration

Western Shape
Hope & Carter
Reg. Sept. 26, 1862
Moreland collection

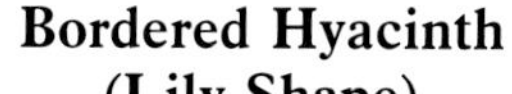

Bordered Hyacinth
(Lily Shape)
W. Baker & Co.,
Fenton
c. 1860
W. & E. Corn
Skinner collection

GRANITE
LILY SHAPE
W&E CORN
BURSLEM

Hyacinth
Wedgwood & Co., Cobridge
c. late 1860s
Wood, Son & Co.
Henry Burgess
John Maddock & Sons 1869 – 1879
Skinner collection

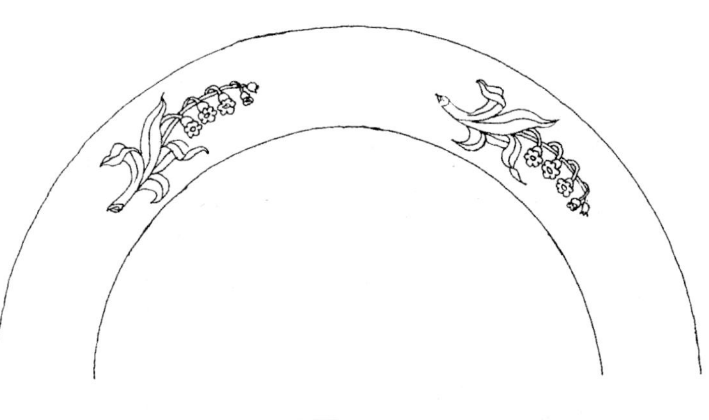

Bell Tracery
(5 divisions)
Holland & Green, Longton
1853-1880
Skinner collection

Tulip Border
Powell & Bishop
1866 – 1878
Volckening and Klein collections

Rope or Chain Borders

Grape Cluster with Chain
(5 divisions)
H. Burgess, Burslem
c. 1865
Erdman collection

(Also see other grape patterns)

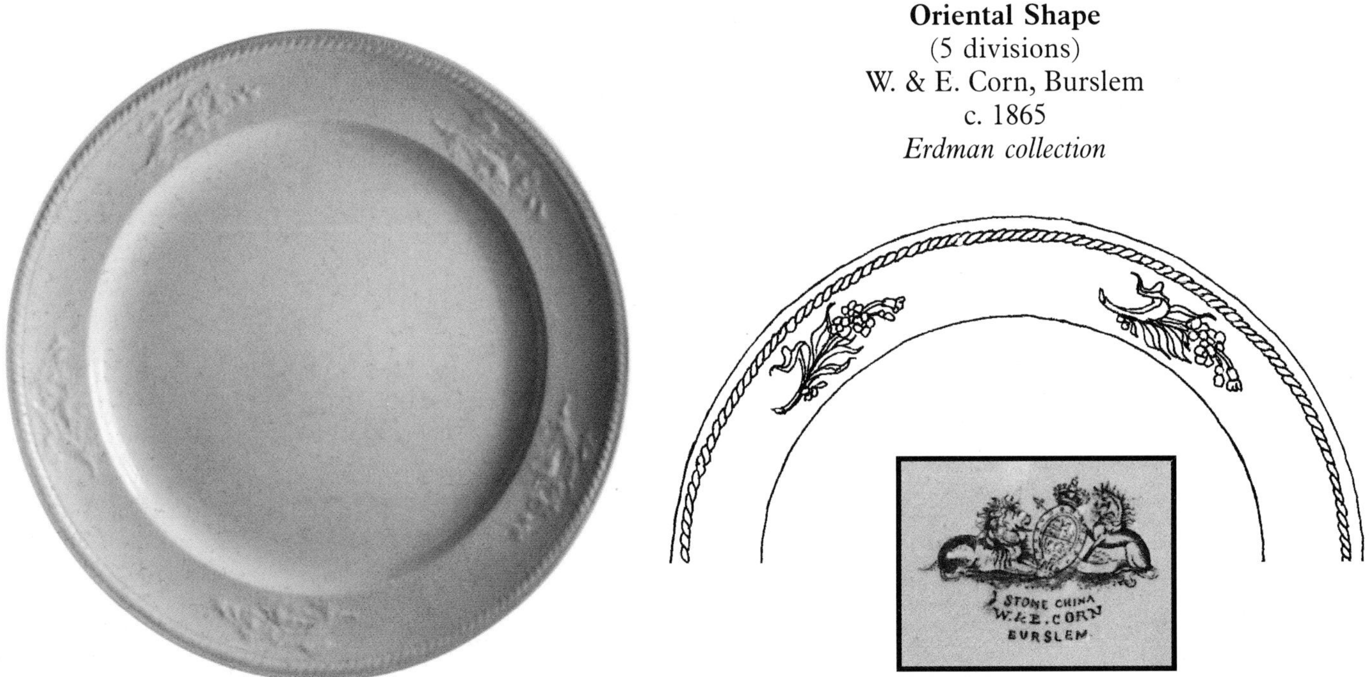

Oriental Shape
(5 divisions)
W. & E. Corn, Burslem
c. 1865
Erdman collection

Flower Sprig with Chain
(5 divisions)
Taylor Bros., Hanley
1862-1871
Secrist collection

Moss Rose
(5 divisions)
J. & G. Meakin
c. 1865
Meakin & Co., Cobridge
Dieringer collection

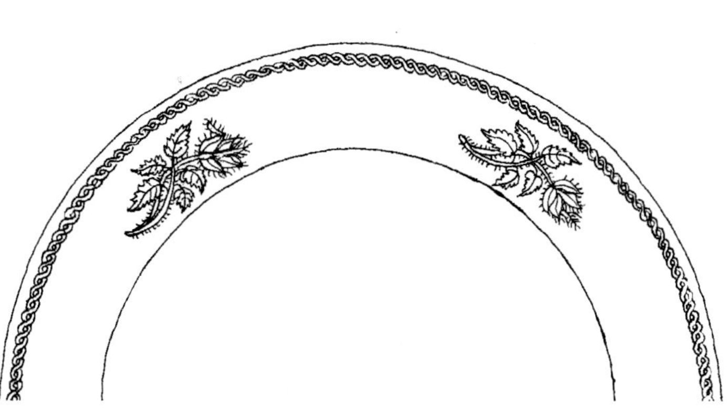

Washington Shape
(5 divisions)
John Meir & Son, Tunstall
Reg. Nov. 3, 1863
Skinner collection

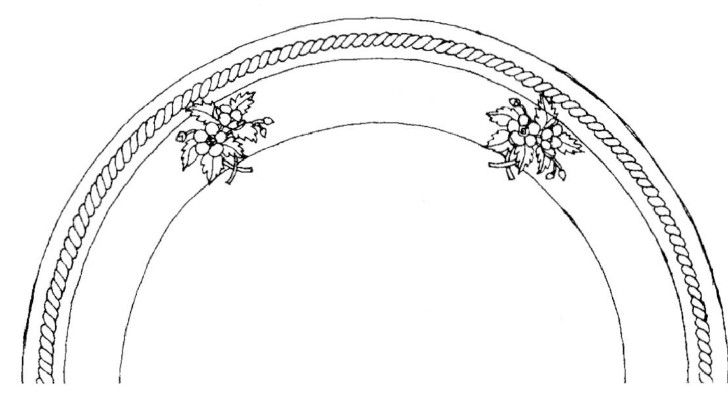

Alternate Sprigs (Washington Shape)
(6 divisions)
Powell & Bishop
c. 1866
(No cable but same flowers as Washington Shape)
Abrams collection

Can be found with
Lustre Band
Rose Lustre
Pomegranate Lustre
Botanical Lustre
decoration

Floral

Forget-Me-Not
(5 divisions)
Henry Alcock
Taylor Bros.
Wood, Rathbone & Co.
c. 1860 – 1869
Skinner collection

Forget-Me-Not
(5 divisions)
E. & C. Challinor, Fenton
1862-1891
Abrams collection

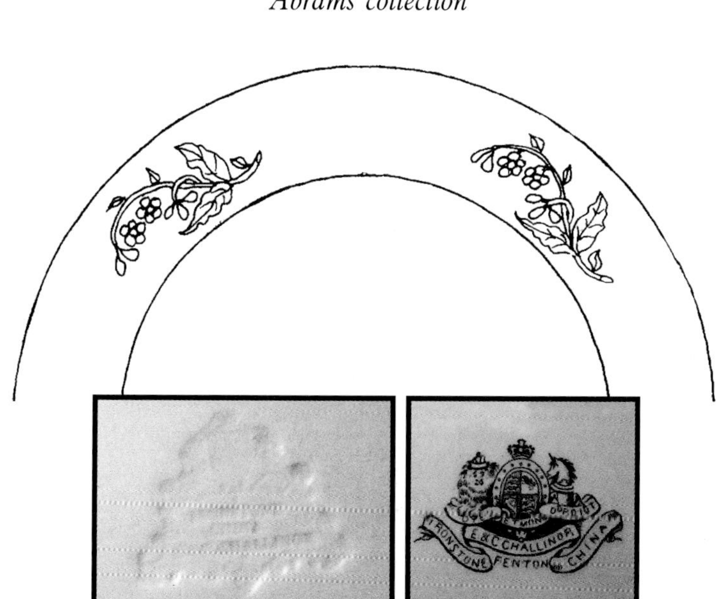

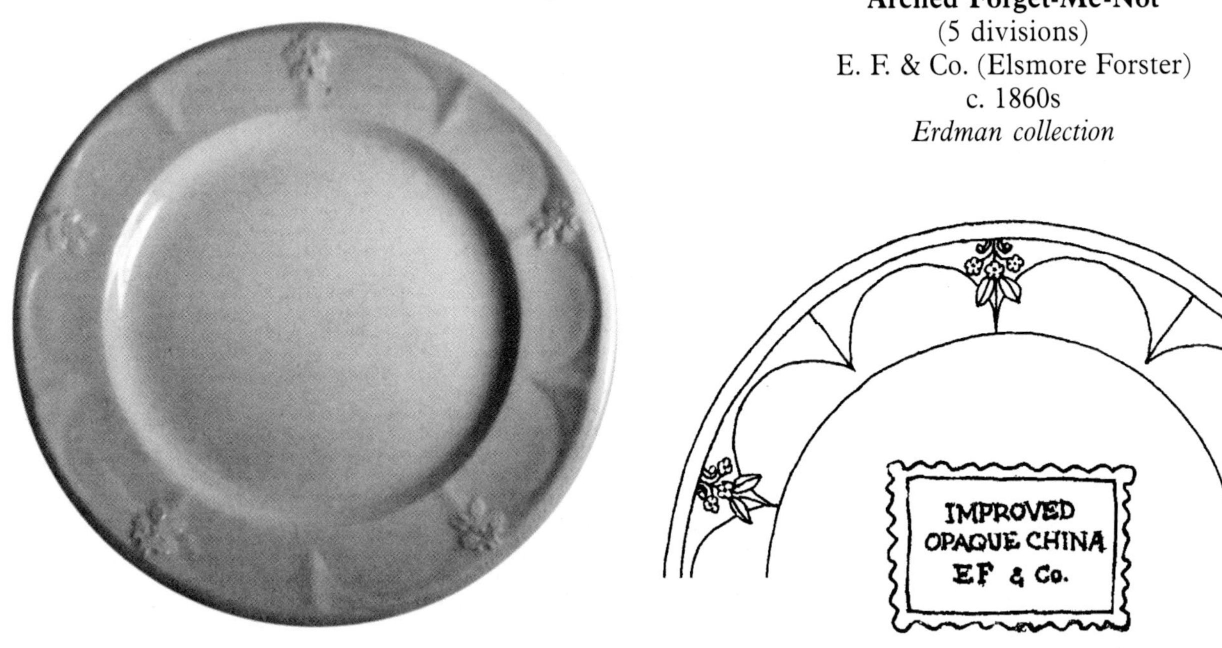

Arched Forget-Me-Not
(5 divisions)
E. F. & Co. (Elsmore Forster)
c. 1860s
Erdman collection

Can be found with
Lustre Band
Botanical Lustre
decoration

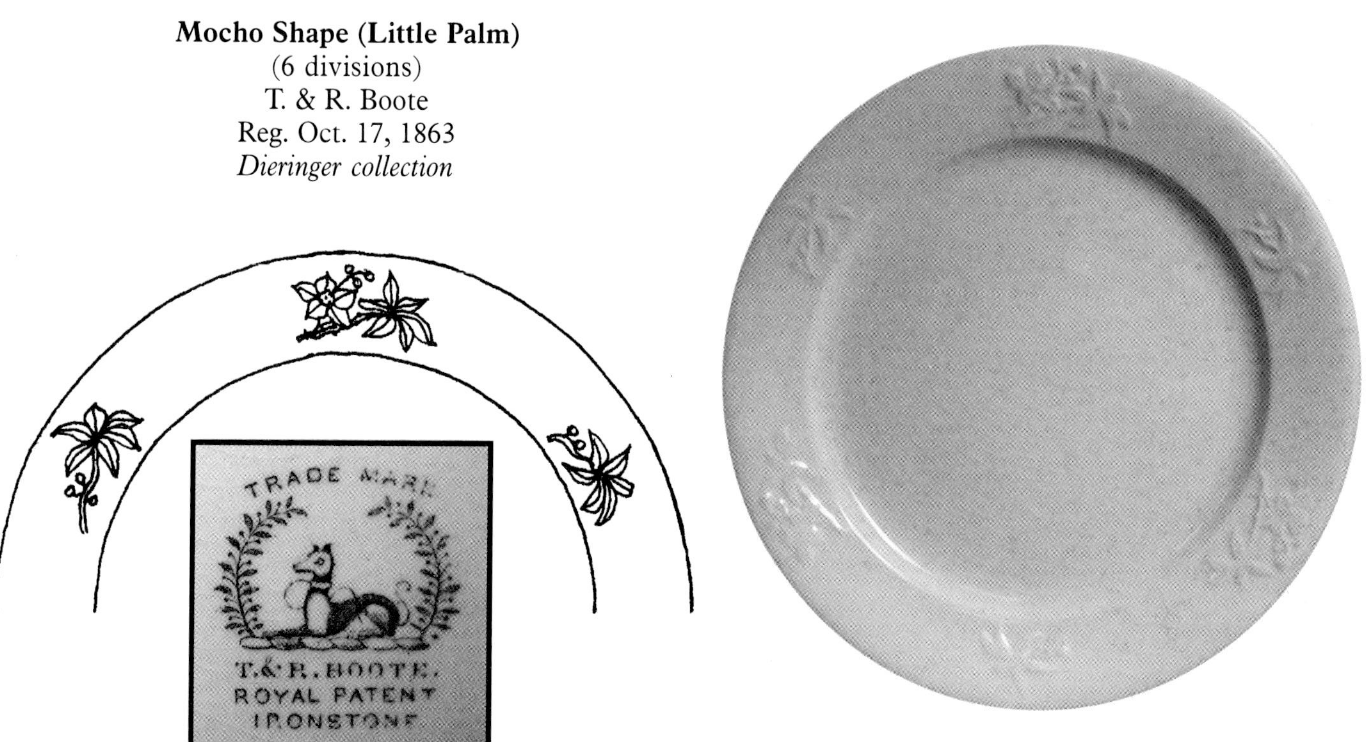

Mocho Shape (Little Palm)
(6 divisions)
T. & R. Boote
Reg. Oct. 17, 1863
Dieringer collection

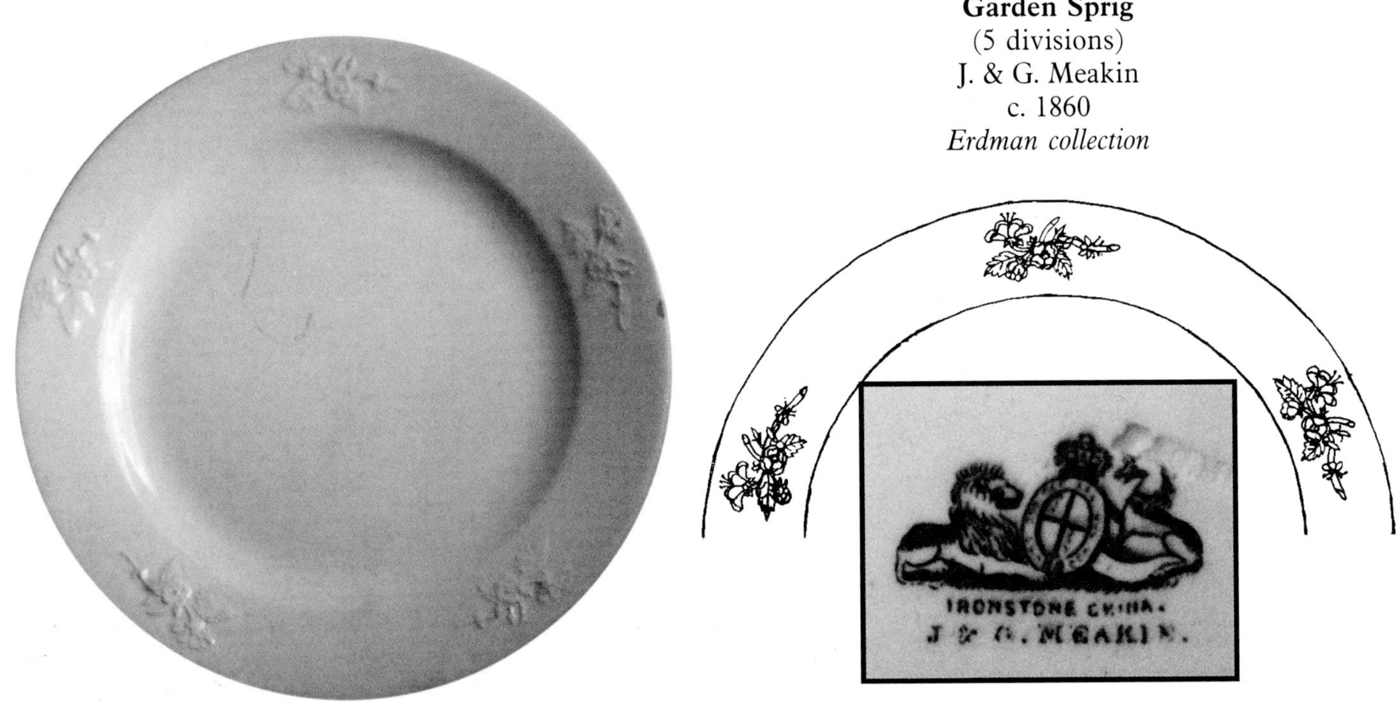

Garden Sprig
(5 divisions)
J. & G. Meakin
c. 1860
Erdman collection

Shaw's Spray
Anthony Shaw, Burslem
c. 1860s
(No photo available)

Hidden Motif
(6 divisions)
Jacob Furnival
(The photo is of a platter. This is the hidden motif that exists on the hollow pieces.)

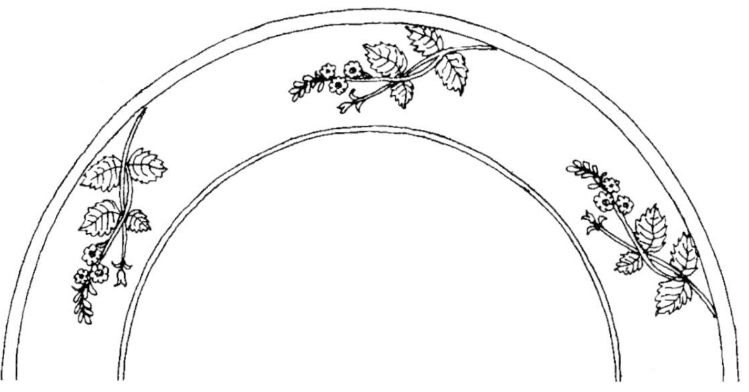

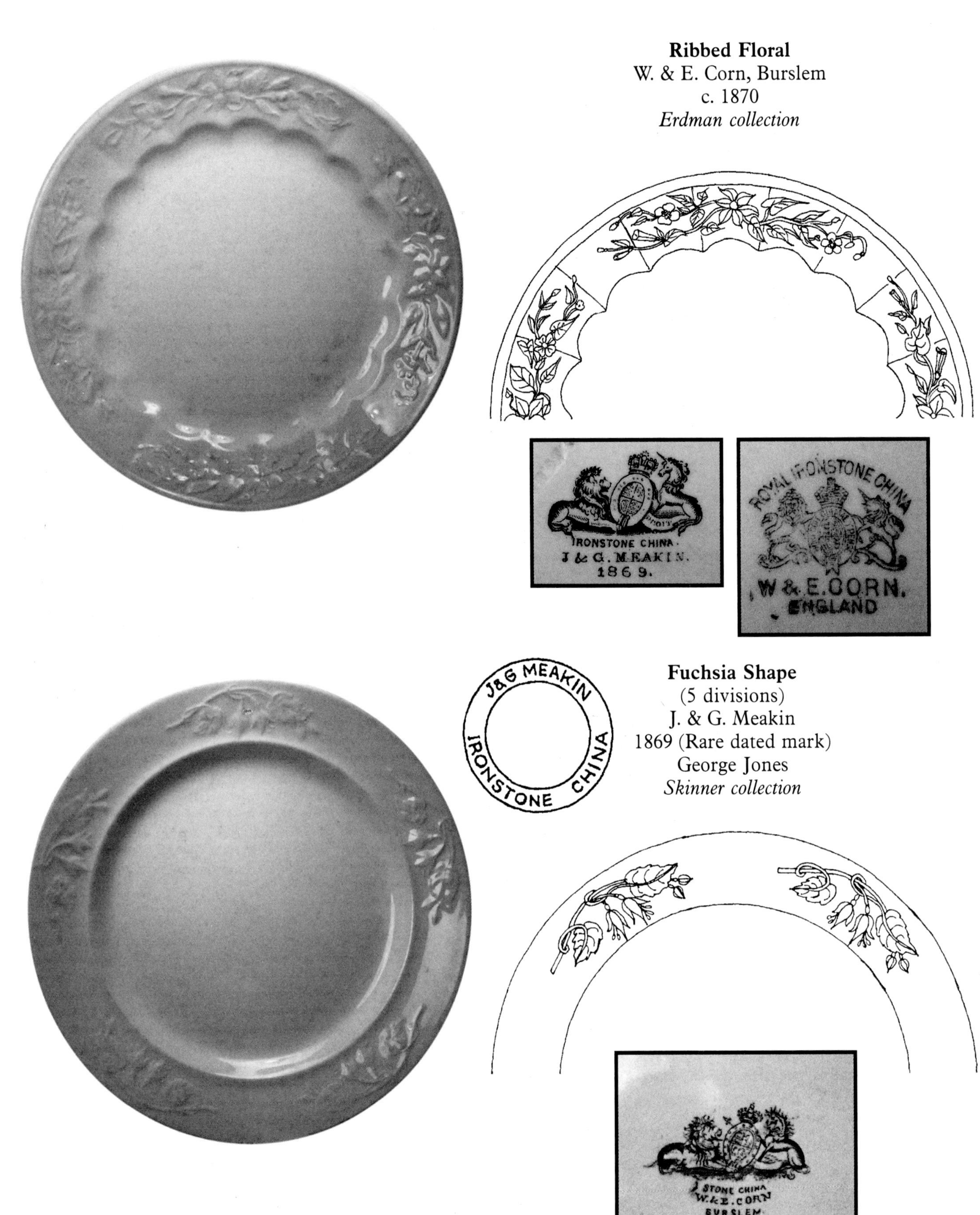

Ribbed Floral
W. & E. Corn, Burslem
c. 1870
Erdman collection

Fuchsia Shape
(5 divisions)
J. & G. Meakin
1869 (Rare dated mark)
George Jones
Skinner collection

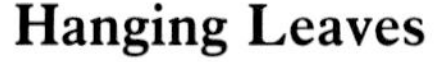

Hanging Leaves
(5 divisions)
Anthony Shaw
c. 1850
Abrams collection

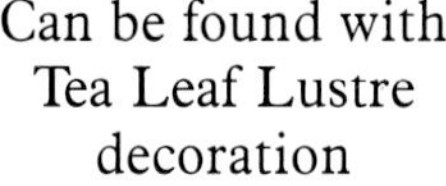

Can be found with
Tea Leaf Lustre
decoration

Bordered Fuchsia
(4 divisions)
Anthony Shaw
1860
Skinner collection

Can be found with
Tea Leaf Lustre decoration

Grape

Grape Cluster
(6 divisions)
Davenport
Reg. May, 27, 1869
Dieringer collection

Vintage Shape
(6 divisions)
W. Adams
Later, E. & C. Challinor
c. 1865
Lautenschlager collection

Can be found with
Tea Leaf Lustre decoration

Grape Wreath on Ribs
Bridgewood & Clark, Burslem
Reg. Sept. 10, 1858 No. 115343
Erdman collection

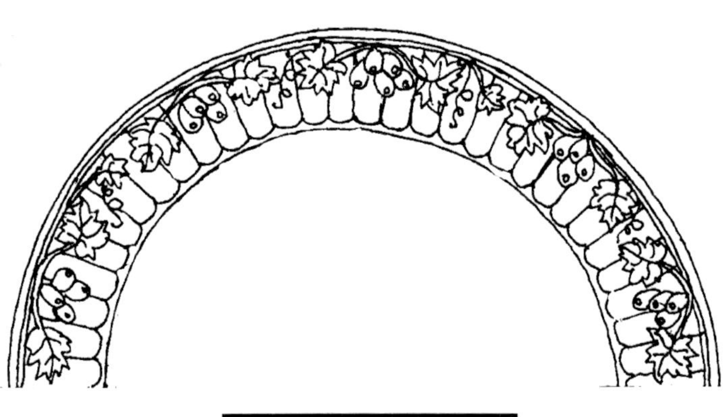

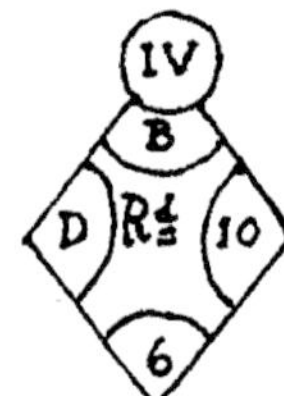

Centennial Shape
W. & E. Corn, Burslem
Reg. Nov. 3, 1874
Pat. No. 286720-2
Skinner collection

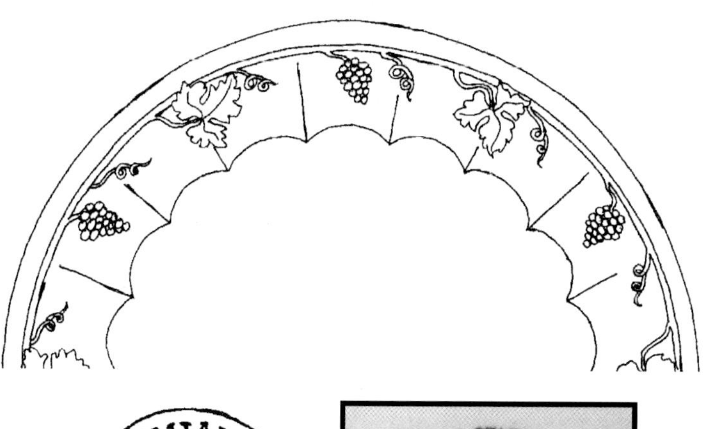

(Also see page 114 for Grape Cluster with Chain)

Wheat

Ceres
(Six grain heads, three kernel rows)
Elsmore & Forster
Reg. Nov. 2, 1859
Turner, Goddard & Co.
Skinner collection

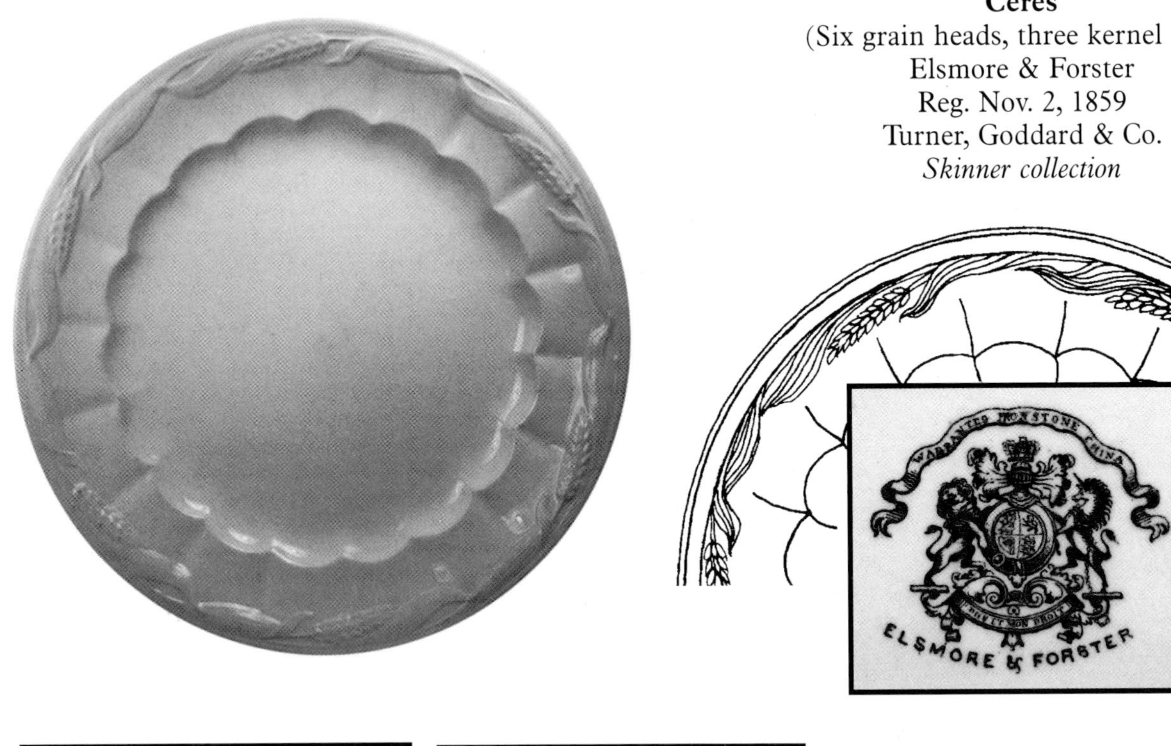

Can be found with
Morning Glory Lustre
and Lustre enhancement
decoration

Wheat and Hops
(Five grain heads two kernel rows)
J. & G. Meakin, later Alfred Meakin,
c. 1875
Baker & Co.
Jacob Furnival
Clementson Bros.
W. Taylor
W. E. Oulsnam & Son
Robert Cochran & Co. (Scotland)
St. Johns Chinaware Co. (Canada)
Hollinshead & Kirkham, Late J.
Wedgwood, Tunstall, c. 1890
Skinner collection

Furnival plates can be found with
Cinquefoil Lustre
decoration

Wheat
Possibly J.F.
(Double wheat heads,
two kernel rows)
Wetherbee collection

The Lorne (Roped Wheat)
Thomas Furnival & Sons,
Cobridge
1878
(No photo available)
Erdman collection

Arched Wheat
R. Cochran & Co.
1856 – 1876
Abrams collection

Can be found with
Copper Lustre
and blue decoration

Wheat and Clover
(3 divisions)
Turner & Tompkinson, Tunstall, 1860 – 1872
Taylor Bros., Hanley, 1862 – 1871
Ford Challinor & Co., Tunstall, 1865 – 1880
Skinner collection

Scotia (Poppy Shape)
F. Jones & Co., Longton
1865-1886
Moreland collection

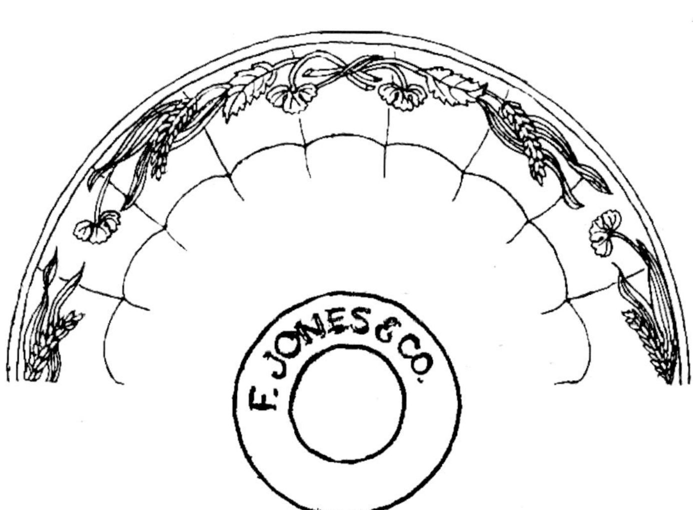

Can be found with
Lustre Band
Pomegranate Lustre
decoration

Prairie Flowers
(5 divisions)
Livesley, Powell & Co., Hanley
1851 – 1866
Powell & Bishop
Skinner collection

Can be found with
Teaberry Lustre
Lustre Band
Cinquefoil Lustre
Coral Lustre
decoration

Prairie Shape
(5 divisions)
J. Clementson, Hanley
(Later, Clementson Bros.)
Reg. Nov. 15, 1861
Skinner collection

Canada
(5 divisions)
Clementson Bros.
Reg. Mar. 20, 1877 #308650-2
Erdman collection

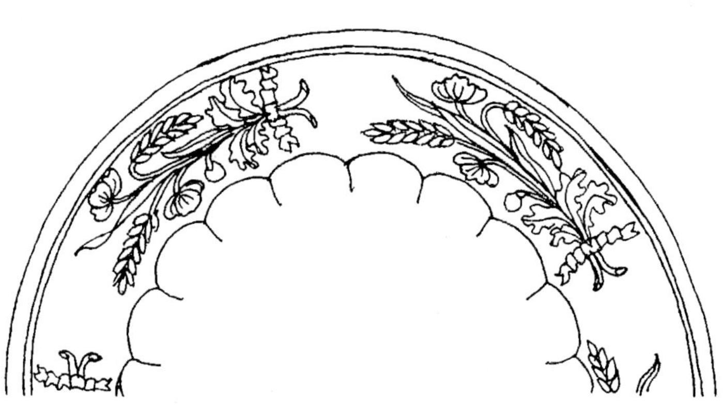

Wheat in the Meadow
Powell & Bishop, Hanley
Reg. Oct. 29, 1869 #235401-2
Skinner collection

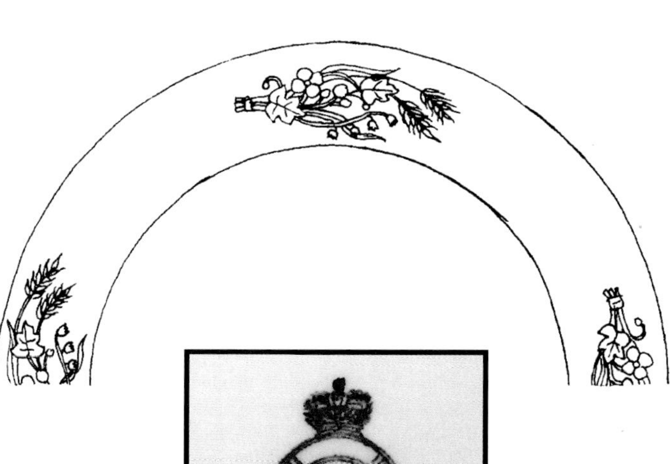

Can be found with
Lustre Band
Rose Lustre
decoration

Corn and Oats (Corn On The Cob Shape)
Davenport, Banks & Co. Reg. Jan. 12, 1863
Wedgwood, Reg. Oct. 31, 1863
Edmund T. Wood
Hollinshead & Kirkham, Reg. Sept. 20, 1876
Skinner collection

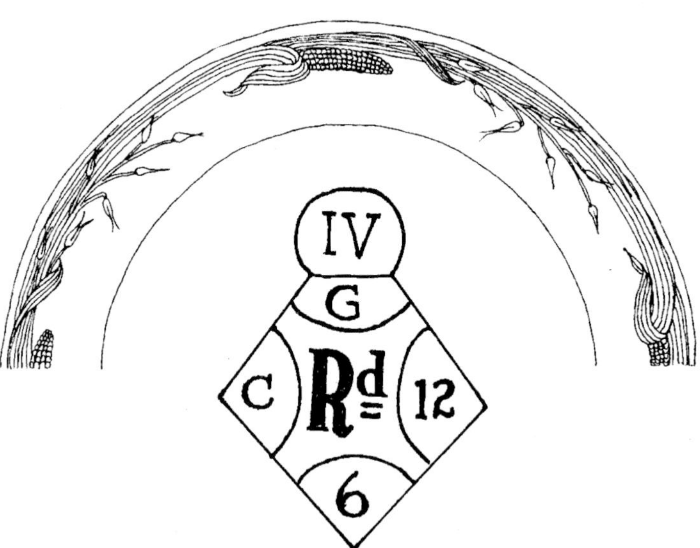

IRONSTONE
J. WEDGWOOD
CHINA

Wheat & Daisy
Wm. Adams & Sons, Tunstall
Bishop & Stonier, Hanley, c. 1890
Johnson Bros., 1883 – 1913
Skinner collection

Wheat & Rose
Alfred Meakin, Tunstall
c. 1890
Skinner collection

Ribbon

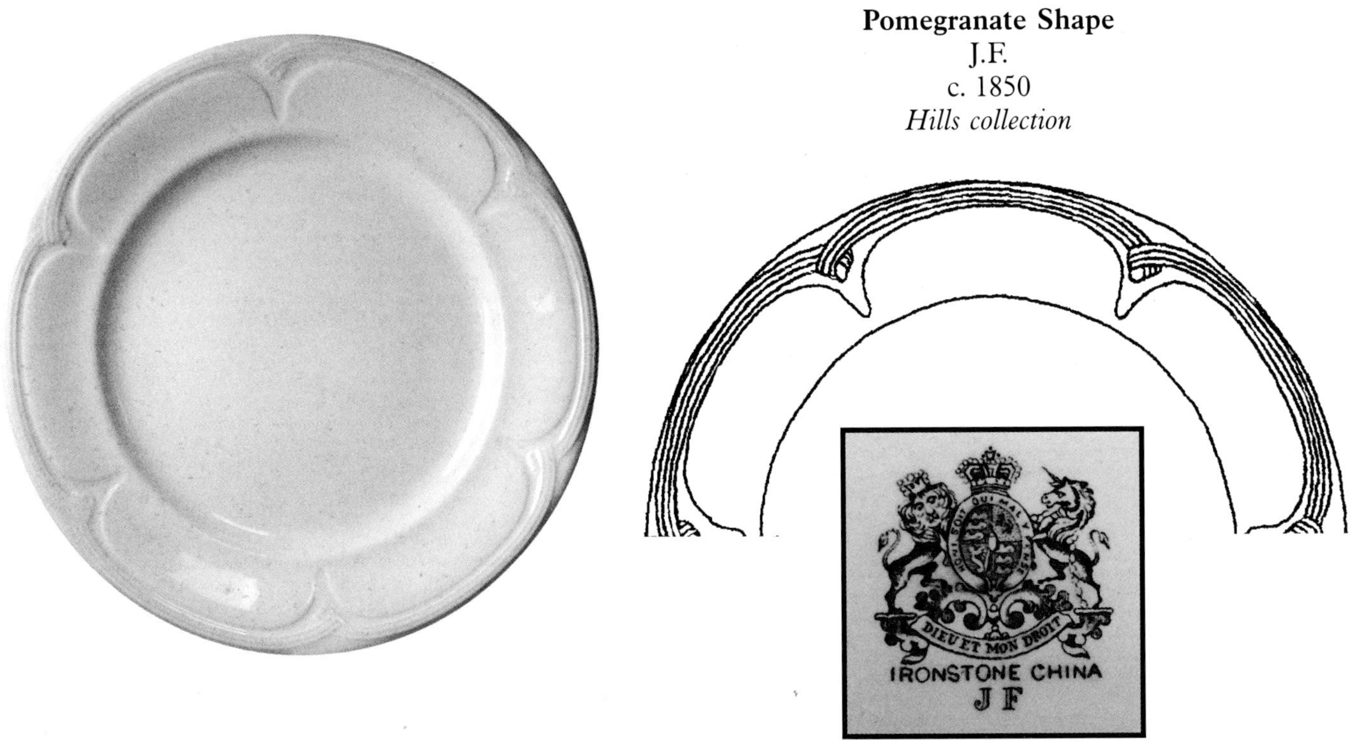

Pomegranate Shape
J.F.
c. 1850
Hills collection

Stafford Shape
S. Alcock & Co. Reg. Sept. 5, 1854
Trent Shape
John Alcock, Reg. June 7, 1855
Henry Alcock, Reg. June 7, 1855
Skinner collection

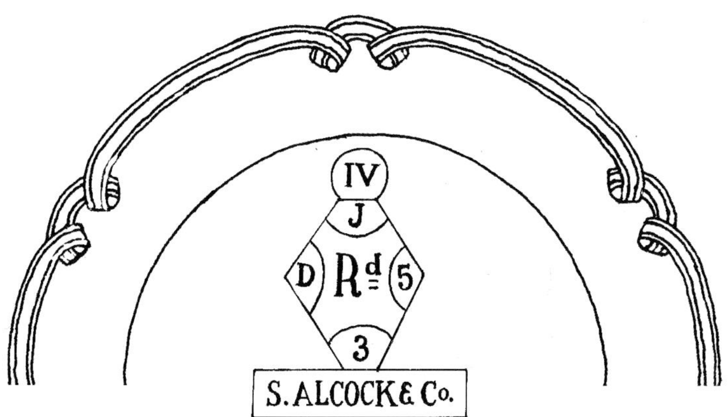

Bow Knot
J. & G. Meakin
c. 1860
Erdman collection

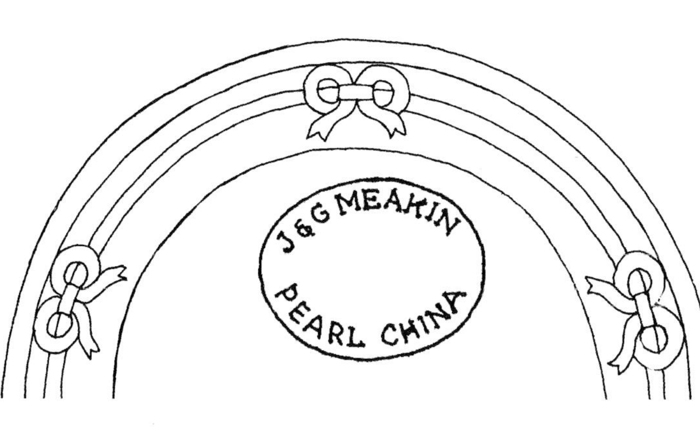

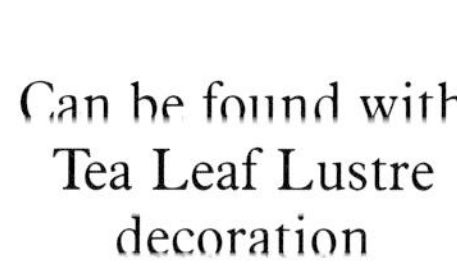
Can be found with
Tea Leaf Lustre
decoration

Nosegay
E. & C. Challinor, Fenton
1842-1867
Baker & Co., Fenton
Erdman collection

Sharon Arch (Erie Shape)
J. Wedgwood, Tunstall
Davenport & Co., Longport
Reg. April 12, 1861
Skinner collection

Leaf & Crossed Ribbon
Livesley & Powell
1851 – 1866
Skinner collection

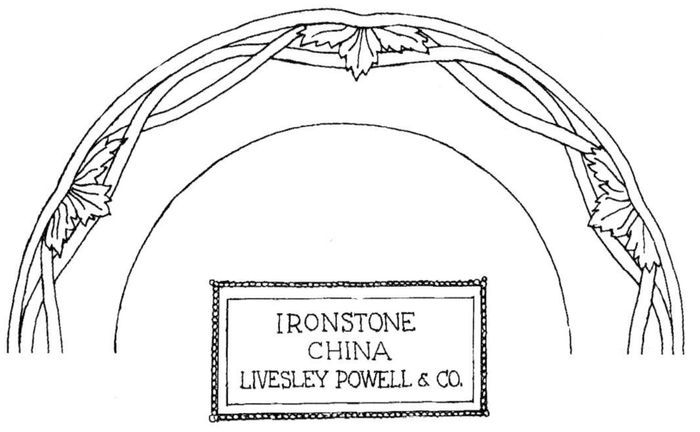

Twisted Ribbon
James Edwards, Dale Hall
Reg. Mar. 21, 1863
Skinner collection

1880-1890 (Late Shapes)

Butterfly and Sunflower
(3 divisions)
Powell & Bishop
c. 1880
Skinner collection

Prunus Blossoms
("Japonism")
(5 divisions)
Henry Alcock & Co. c.
1880s
(No photo available)

Fuschia with Band
(3 divisions)
Mellor, Taylor & Co., Burslem
1880 – 1904
Skinner collection

Basket Weave with Band
Alfred Meakin, Tunstall
A. J. Wilkinson, England
1880s
Riley collection

Flower Garden Border
(6 divisions)
W. H. Grindley & Co., Tunstall
c. 1880
Skinner collection

Medallion Sprig
(4 divisions)
Powell & Bishop
c. 1880s
Skinner collection

Ruffeled Edge
Thos. Hughes & Son
After 1884
Miller collection

Can be found with
Tea Leaf Lustre
decoration

Pie Crust (Blanket Stitch)
J. & G. Meakin, Hanley
c. 1880s
Henry Alcock
Skinner collection

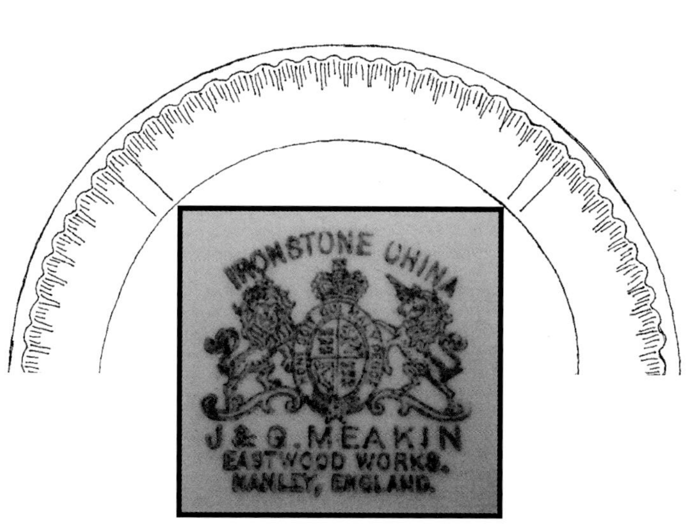

Can be found with
Tea Leaf Lustre
decoration

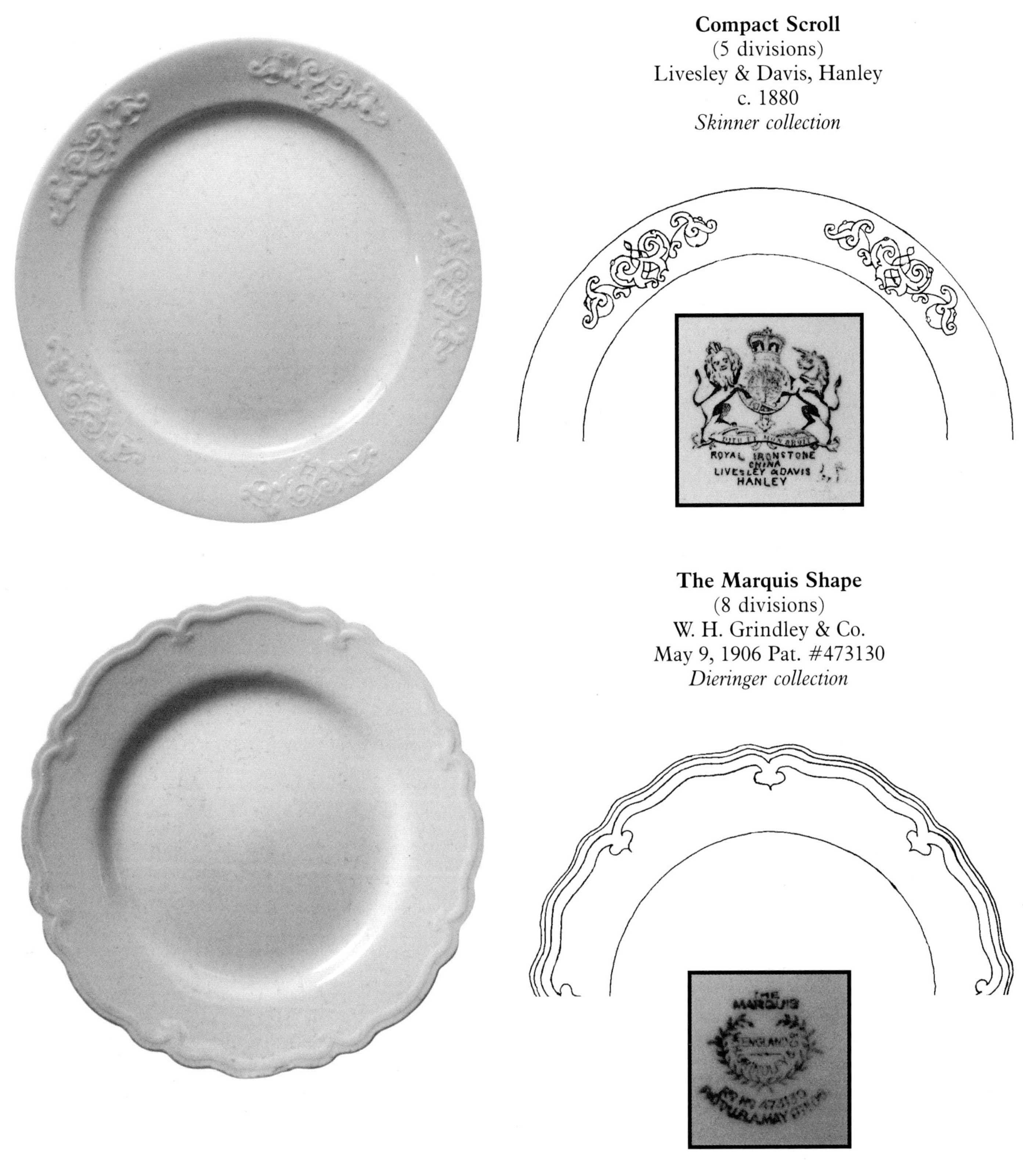

Compact Scroll
(5 divisions)
Livesley & Davis, Hanley
c. 1880
Skinner collection

The Marquis Shape
(8 divisions)
W. H. Grindley & Co.
May 9, 1906 Pat. #473130
Dieringer collection

Acanthus
(6 divisions)
Johnson Bros.
c. 1880
Erdman collection
Can be found with
Tea Leaf Lustre
decoration

Beaded Rings
(8 divisions)
Johnson Bros.
After 1890

Sea Shells

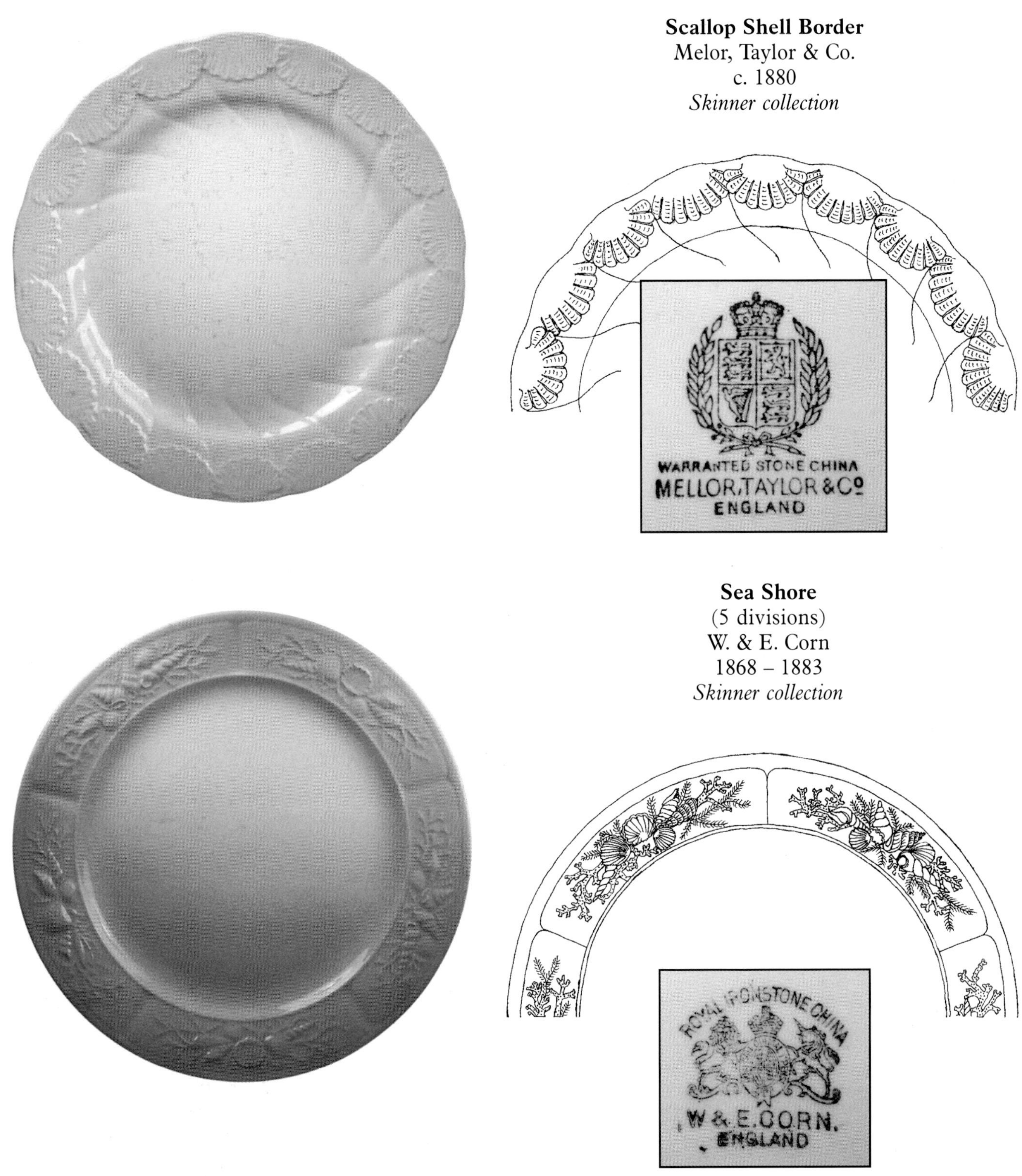

Scallop Shell Border
Melor, Taylor & Co.
c. 1880
Skinner collection

Sea Shore
(5 divisions)
W. & E. Corn
1868 – 1883
Skinner collection

Fish and Shell Plate
(4 divisions)
Minton & Co.
Reg. Jan. 21, 1869
Dieringer collection

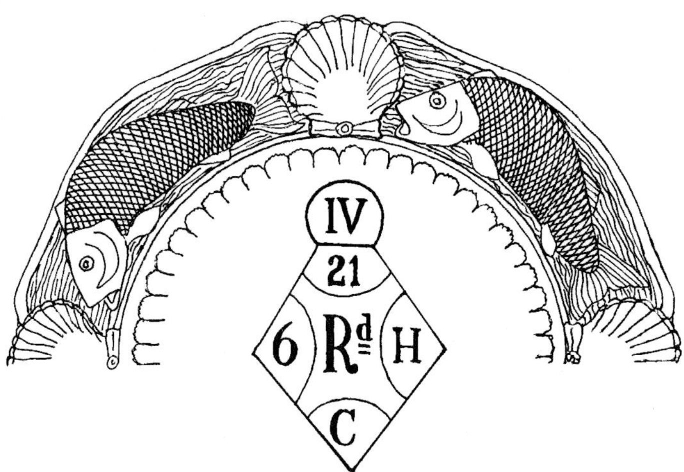

Over-All Embossed

Lily Pad
Pankhurst & Co.
1852 – 1882
Dieringer collection

Flower Blanket (Geranium)
Jacob Furnival
1845 – 1870
Skinner collection

Fruit Garden
Barrow & C0
1853 – 1856
Livesley & Powell
1851 – 1865
Skinner collection
Can be found with
Lustre enhancement

Fruit Garden
Burleigh Ware
c. 1990s
This is evidence that Davenport made a similar tea service plate. Burleigh has reproduced many early ironstone patterns. Fortunately, they are very responsible about marking their pieces.

Shapes to be Looking For...

Plates in the following known ironstone shapes were not found to illustrate in this work. If a reader finds one of them, please send the authors a photograph in care of the publisher, and we will include it in a later edition of this book. To help in identifying them, drawings of some border motifs found on pieces other than a plate are shown here.

Shape Name	Potter	Registration Date
Baltimore Shape 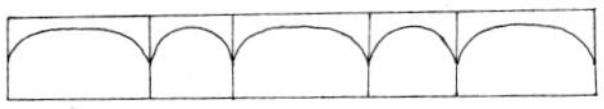	Brougham & Mayer	
Dominion 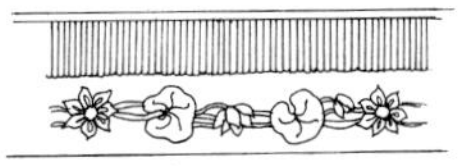	W. Baker & Co.	Reg. June 13, 1877
Florentine	C. & W. K. Harvey	Reg. July 16, 1850
Flower Garden Border 	W. H. Grindley	
Garibaldi Shape	T. & R. Boote	Reg. Nov. 23, 1860
Garland	Cockson, Chetwyn & Co.	
Lily Shape/Cala Lily 	H. Burgess	
Meadow Bouquet	W. Baker & Co.	
Mobile Shape	G. Bowers/ W. Adams/ J. Heath	Reg. by Ralph Scragg (Modeler) Apr. 18, 1856
Napier Shape	Bridgwood & Son	
Nut with Bud	John Meir & Son	
Pacific Shape	Elsmore & Forster	Reg. Feb. 20, 1871
Ribboned Oak	W. & E. Corn	
Scrolled Border 	Bridgewood & Son	
Summer Garden 	George Jones	
Tracery	Johnson Bros	
Trailing Ivy	John Maddock & Son	
Trumpet Vine 	Liddle, Elliot & Son	Reg. Sept. 18, 1865
Wheat Harvest 	John Alcock	
White Oak and Acorn	Holland & Green	
Winterberry 	Edward Clarke	

Copper and Gold Lustre

Tea Leaf and More...Copper Lustre Decorative Motifs on White Ironstone

Dale Abrams

It was not long after the turn of the nineteenth century, English potters developed and introduced ironstone china, primarily for export to North America. Although William and John Turner patented the first of the inexpensive and durable opaque earthenwares in 1800 their pottery went bankrupt in 1806. Other manufacturers introduced similar wares including Spode, Davenport and Hicks & Meigh, but it was not until 1813 when Charles Mason made public his "Patent Ironstone China" that white ironstone became a household word. Mason became the most well-known of the early ironstone potters and held an exclusive patent to the formula for fourteen years. By the time his patent expired mny of the other Staffordshire potters had developed formulas of their own.

Early white ironstone production was genereally sold after being decorated with any of a number of motifs-- copies of Oriental patterns, historical blue, flow blue, mulberry, over-all lustre applications, gaudy designs and numerous others. It was in the 1840s that plain undecorated white ironstone began to be sold in quantity to the world market. All-white ironstone was a huge success with the North American consumer and sold well for many of the dozens of potters whose output was marketed in the States and Canada.

Consumer tastes are ever-changing and nearly concurrent withthe popularity of undecorated white ironstone an new trend took hold. Some potters began to enhance their wares with various copper lustre effects and motifs. Beginning simply with the addition of copper-colored lustre bands to pieces, the decorators eventually employed a variety of fanciful floral and geometric motifs, many of which are shown in the following chart. The copper lustre treatment was obtained by the addition of gold or copper oxide to the glazeswhich the potter used in the decorating phase of the firing. Copper lustre decorated ware is generally characterized by thin banding around the top and base rims of pieces, lustre accents to handles and finials, and often one of the motifs shown added prominently to flat and hollowware pieces.

In the mid-1850s Anthony Shaw introduced a new design that was destined to take the consumer market by storm-- Tea Leaf. For almost fifty years, Tea Leaf-decorated ironstone was a favorite of the American family. More than thirty English potters eventually adopted the Tea Leaf motif and used it on over one hundred body styles (shapes). While Tea Leaf popularity waned in the late 1800s, American potters eagerly entered the Tea Leaf market and eventually over twenty-five American manufacturers also employed the Tea Leaf (or close variant) motif. American production was, however, relatively short-lived and, with the exception of a brief resurgence in the 1960s, copper lustre decorated white ironstone did not at the time recapture the hearts of the American consumer as it had their great-great-grandmothers a hundred years earlier.

Today's collectors eagerly search out Tea Leaf and all of its variant motifs, and copper lustre decorated whit ironstone has once again become prized for its durability, beauty, simplicity, craft and style.

For more information about Tea Leaf and copper lustre decorated ironstone china, or for information about the Tea Leaf Club International, contact Dale Abrams at 960 Bryden Road, Columbus, Ohio 43205, phone 614-258-5258.

Plain Shapes Sometimes Touched with Lustre

Late 1870s and 1880s

Shape Name	Potter	Lustre Decorative Motifs on White Ironstone
	Tea Leaf	
Bamboo	A. Meakin, Grindley	
Bullet	Anthony Shaw	
Cable	Various Potters	
Coronet	Anthony Shaw	
Daisy	Anthony Shaw	
Daisy 'n Chain	A. J. Wilkinson	
Daisy 'n Tulip (Late Tulip)	Wedgwood & Co.	
Fishook (Gentle Square)	A. Meakin	
Gentle Square	Furnival	
Hawthorn	A. J. Wilkinson	
Heavy Square	Clementson Bros.	
Hexagon	A. Shaw	
Jumbo	Henry Alcock	
Lion's Head	Mellor, Taylor & Co.	
Little Cable	Thomas Furnival	
Peerless	John Edwards	
Plain Round	Many Potters	
Royal (impressed)	John Edwards	
Scroll	Alfred Meakin	
Simple Square	Many Potters	
Simplicity	Shaw, Powell & Bishop	
Sunburst	A. J. Wilkinson	
Victory (impressed)	John Edwards	
	Teaberry	
Beaded Band	Clementson Bros.	
Elegance	Clementson Bros.	
Grape Vine	Clementson Bros.	
Heavy Square	Clementson Bros.	
	Morning Glory	
Draped Leaf	W. Baker & Co.	
Crystal	Elsmore & Forster	
Richelieu	James Wileman	

Tea Leaf

Teaberry

Morning Glory

Shape Name	Potter	Lustre Decorative Motifs on White Ironstone

Tobacco Leaf / Pepper Leaf

Shape Name	Potter
Crystal	Elsmore & Forster
Fanfare	Elsmore & Forster

Tobacco Leaf

Pepperleaf

Copper Lustre Band

Shape Name	Potter
Jumbo	Henry Alcock
Lily of the Valley	Anthony Shaw
Pear	Anthony Shaw

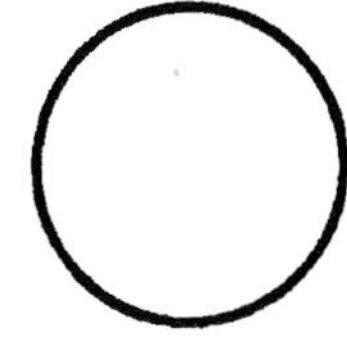

Lustre Band

Luster Rose

Shape Name	Potter
Simplicity	Powell & Bishop

Rose

Other Lustre Decorative Motifs on White Ironstone

Pre-Tea Leaf

Reverse Teaberry

Pomegranate

Cinquefoil

Coral

Pinwheel

Thistle and Berry

Botanicals (Various Motifs)

Scallops

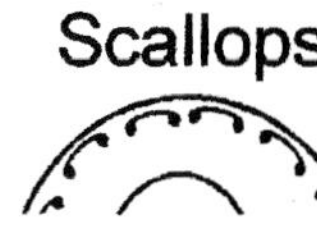

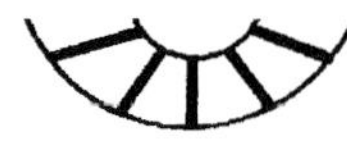

Spokes

Bibliography

Cushion, J. P., *Pocket Book of British Ceramic Marks*, Farber and Farber, Fourth Edition, London, 1994.

Godden, Geoffrey A., *Encyclopaedia of British Pottery and Porcelain Marks*, Barre and Jenkins Ltd., London, 1993.

Godden, Geoffrey A., *Goddens's Guide to Ironstone, Stone and Granite Wares*, Antique Collectors' Club Ltd., Woodbridge, Suffolk, 1999.

Heaivilin, Annise D., *Grandma's Tea Leaf Ironstone*, Wallace Homestead, Des Moines, Iowa, 1981.

Kowalsky, Arnold A. and Dorothy E., *Encyclopedia of Marks on American, English and European Earthenware, Ironstone, and Stoneware (1780-1980)*, Schiffer Publishing Ltd., Atglen, Pennsylvania, 1999.

Upchurch, Nancy J., *Tea Leaf Handbook*, The Tea Leaf Club International, 1995.

Wetherbee, Jean, *White Ironstone: A Collector's Guide*, Antique Trader Books, Dubuque, Iowa, 1996.

White Ironstone China Association, Inc., *Newsletter*.

Price Guide For Plates With Copper Lustre Motifs

Key to abbreviations:

BOT=Botanical	PTL=PreTea Leaf
CNQ=Cinquefoil	ROS=Rose
COR=Coral	RTB=Reverse Teaberry
LB=Lustre Band	SCA=Scallops
MG=Morning Glory	SPO=Spokes
OTHER=Other Motifs or Lustre Applications	T&B=Thistle & Berry
PEP=Pepperleaf	TB=Teaberry
PIN=Pinwheel	TL=TeaLeaf
POM=Pomegranate	TOB=Tobacco Leaf

Acanthus TL $25-$50
Arched Forget-Me-Not LB Under $25, BOT $75-100
Arched Wheat OTHER $75-100
Augusta Shape LB $25-50, TB $75-100

Balanced Vine LB $25-50, TB $75-100
Bamboo TL Under $25
Basketweave TL Under $25
Beaded Band TB $25-50
Bellflower TL Under $25
Berry Cluster LB $25-50, TB $100+
Blanket Stitch (Pie Crust) TL Under$25
Bordered Fuchsia TL $50-75
Brocade TL $25-50
Bullet TL Under $25

Cable TL and LB Under $25, MG and POM $25-50
Ceres OTHER $50-75
Chelsea TL Under $25
Chinese Shape LB $25-50, TL and OTHER $50-75, TB $75-100
Cockscomb Handle TB $50-75, LB Under $25
Columbia Shape LB and MG $25-50, TOB $75-100
Coronet TL Under $25
Crewel TL Under $25
Crystal Shape LB Under $25, MG $25 50, PEP and TOB $50-75

Daisy TL Under $25
Daisy & Tulip TL Under $25
Daisy & Chain TL Under $25
Dallas Shape LB $25-50
Draped Leaf MG $25-50

Fanfare TOB $50-75
Favorite TL Under $25
Fig Cousin TL Under $25
Fishhook TL and OTHER Under $25
Fleur-de-Lis Chain TL $25-50
Fleur-de-Lys TL $25-50
Full Ribbed MG $25-50

Gentle Square TL Under $25
Golden Scroll TL and LB Under $25
Gothic Classic TB LB and PIN $25-50, SCA and SPO $50-75, T&B $75-100
Gothic Full Paneled TB, LB, MG and PIN $25-50
Gothic Many Paneled TL, TB and LB $25-50
Grand Loop LB $25-50, TB, CIN and OTHER $50-75, BOT $100+
Grape Octagon TB, LB, PIN and POM $25-50, PTL, SCA,T&B and OTHER $50-75
Grape Vine TB $25-50
Grenade Shape TL Under $25

Hanging Leaves TL $25-50
Hawthorn TL Under $25

Heavy Square TL and TB $50-75
Hexagon TL Under $25
Hill Shape (Medallion Scroll) TB, LB and COR $100+
Huron Shape TL and LB $50-75
Hyacinth (Cochran's Ring) PTL $100+

Jumbo TL Under $25

Laurel Wreath (Victory Shape) OTHER $75-100
Lily-of-the-Valley TL and LB $25-50
Lion's Head TL Under $25
Little Cable TL Under $25

Maidenhair Fern TL $25-50

Nautilus LB $50-75
New York Shape TB, LB and OTHER $50-75, COR $100+
Niagara Fan TL and LB $50-75
Niagara Shape LB, PIN, POM and OTHER $50-75, PTL $75-100

Paneled Grape TB, LB, CNQ, PIN and OTHER $50-75, BOT $100+
Pear TL Under $25, LB 50-75
Peerless Shape (Feather) TL $25-50
Plain Round TL Under $25, MG $25-50, BOT $75-100
Polonaise TL Under $25
Portland Shape LB and MG $50-75, RTB $75-100
Prairie Flowers LB and POM $50-75
Prairie Shape TB, LB and CNQ $50-75, COR $100+

Quartered Rose TB, LB, PIN and OTHER $50-75

Richelieu Shape MG $25-50
Ring O'Hearts TB, LB and PIN $50-75
Rococo MG $25-50
Rondeau TL Under 25
Royal TL Under $25
Ruffled Edge TL Under $25

Scroll TL Under $25
Senate Shape TL Under $25
Shield TL Under $25
Simple Pear TL Under $25
Simplicity TL Under $25, ROS $25-50
Simple Square TL Under $25
Square Ridged TL Under $25
Sunburst TL Under $25
Swags & Scroll LB and OTHER $50-75, PTL $75-100

Tulip Shape (Little Scroll) LB, TOB and OTHER $50-75

Victory (Dolphin) TL Under $25
Vintage TL $100+

Walled Octagon LB $50-75
Washington Shape (Alt Sprigs) LB, POM and ROS $50-75
Wheat CNQ $50-75
Wheat in the Meadow LB and ROS $50-75
Woodland TL $25-50
Wrapped Sydenham TL, LB and OTHER $50-75, PTL and SCA $75-100

Index of Shape Names and Price Guide to White Ironstone Plates

The value of a plate is determined by how old or rare it is, the quality of its design, the potting (especially the embossed detail), its glazing (blue-white is preferred), its condition, and the popularity of the shape. All prices given here are approximate and are for 9" to10 ½" supper or dinner plates, which are in perfect condition, with good embossed detail: no crazing, cracks, or chips, any of which diminish the value considerably. An average dinner plate is $30.- $35. Most collectors use their plates and do not buy them with any flaws. Popular Shapes are collected to build sets, making them harder to find and higher priced. Others (Baltic, Grape Octagon, and Columbia Shape) were licensed by the modeler to many manufacturers, making them now easy to find and lower priced. Comparable soup plates are harder to find and are a little higher.

Page	White Ironstone Plates	$
143	Acanthus	20
89	Acorn	25
62	Adams Scallop	75
48	Adriatic Shape	35
65	Alcocks' Unnamed Shape	30
36	Alternate Loops	35
111	Alternate Sprigs	35
9	Amarican Shape	under 25
98	Arbor Vine	30
84	Asia Shape	40
81	Athenia	35
80	Athena Shape	35
88	Athens Shape	30
44	Atlantic Shape	50
37	Augusta Shape	35
116	Arched Forget Me Not	35
128	Arched Wheat	50-75
90	Balanced Vine	35
15	Ball & Stick	45
60	Baltic Shape	35
9	Bar & Chain	under 25
139	Basketweave with Band	35
143	Beaded Rings	20
107	Bellflower	35
111	Bell Tracery	35
9	Berlin Gothic	50-75
66	Berlin Swirl	65
42	Berry Cluster	40
19	Boote's Gothic	60
51	Boote's 1851 decagon	65
51	Boote's 1851 round	60

Page	White Ironstone Plates	$
121	Bordered Fuchsia	45
103	Bordered Gooseberry	35
109	Bordered Hyacinth	45
135	Bow Knot	35
9	Britannia	under 25
19	Brownfield's Gothic	50
101	Budded Vine	30
138	Butterfly & Sunflower	40
9	Cable & Ring	under 25
131	Canada	45
125	Centennial Shape	35
126	Ceres Shape (E & F)	65
126	Ceres Shape (T &G)	50
9	Chain Of Tulips	under 25
38	Chinese, Shaw	35
26	Chinese Shape	35
9	Classic Shape	under 25
9	Clover	under 25
107	Cochran's Ring	45
50	Columbia Shape	35
142	Compact Scroll	25
24	Coral (Fluted Pearl)	65
59	Cora Shape	45
132	Corn & Oats	60
9	Crystal Shape	under 25
17	Curved Gothic	100+
60	Dallas Shape	40
27	DeSoto Shape	35
9	Dolphin (Victory)	under 25
58,59	Double Sydenham	45
73	Dover Shape	45

Page	White Ironstone Plates	$
12	Plain Berlin	25
8	Plain Round	under 25
9	Plain Scallop (Crystal)	under 25
9	Plain Uplift	under 25
134	Pomegranate Shape	35
129	Poppy (Scotia Shape)	45
31,32	Portland Shapes	55
92	Potomac Shape	50
130	Prairie Flowers	45
130	Prairie Shape	45
49	President Shape	45
64	Prize Bloom	50
64	Prize Puritan	50
138	Prunus Blossoms	35
35	Quartered Rose	35
72	Ribbed Chain	45
70	Ribbed Fern	35
120	Ribbed Floral	35
71	Ribbed Raspberry w/Bloom	55
9	Richeleiu Shape	under 25
25	Ridgway / Morley (unnamed paneled shape)	35
47	Ring 'O Hearts	35
9	Ring & Cable	under 25
45	Rolling Star	55
9	Rondeau	under 25
89	Round Acorn	25
29	Round Scallop	60
9,10	Royal Shape	under 25
141	Ruffled Edge	25
61	Scalloped Decagon / Cambridge Shape	60
144	Scallop Shell Border	35
37	Scragg's (unnamed shape)	35
68	Scrolled Bubble	35
144	Sea Shore	50
9	Seine Shape	under 25
9,10	Senate Shape	under 25
12	Sevres Shape	25
136	Sharon Arch	40
119	Shaw's Spray	25
9	Simplicity	under 25

Page	White Ironstone Plates	$
35	Split Pod	35
135	Stafford Shape	55
102	Starflower	30
65	St Louis Shape	35
53	Sydenham Shape (decagon)	75
52	Sydenham Shape (round)	65
128	The Lorne Shape (Roped Wheat)	35
142	The Marquis Shape	25
89	Tiny Oak & Acorn	25
135	Trent Shape	55
14	Triple Border / Challinor's Pear	35
29	True Scallop	65
85	Tulip Shape	35
111	Tulip Border	45
87	Tuscan	35
86	Twin Leaves	35
137	Twisted Ribbon	35
13	Union Shape (T.&R. Boote)	25
43	Venables (unnamed shape)	35
74	Victor Shape (F. Jones)	55
9	Victory (Dolphin)	under 25
75	Victory Shape / (Laurel Wreath)	65
97	Vine with Coral Bells	35
123	Vintage Shape	35
39	Virgina Shape	30
16	Walled Octagon	60
114	Washington Shape	45
108	Western Shape	35
128	Wheat	25
129	Wheat & Clover	60
133	Wheat & Daisy	20
127	Wheat & Hops	45
131	Wheat in the Meadow	25
133	Wheat & Rose	20
99	Winding Vine	35
63	Wooliscroft's Gothic	35
58,59	Wrapped Sydenham	45
96	Wreath of Leaves	50

Index of Potters